I'm OK – You're Not

I'M OK –
YOU'RE
NOT

The Message We're Sending Unbelievers
and Why We Should Stop

by John Shore

NAVPRESS®

BRINGING TRUTH TO LIFE

OUR GUARANTEE TO YOU

We believe so strongly in the message of our books that we are making this quality guarantee to you. If for any reason you are disappointed with the content of this book, return the title page to us with your name and address and we will refund to you the list price of the book. To help us serve you better, please briefly describe why you were disappointed. Mail your refund request to: NavPress, P.O. Box 35002, Colorado Springs, CO 80935.

The Navigators is an international Christian organization. Our mission is to advance the gospel of Jesus and His kingdom into the nations through spiritual generations of laborers living and discipling among the lost. We see a vital movement of the gospel, fueled by prevailing prayer, flowing freely through relational networks and out into the nations where workers for the kingdom are next door to everywhere.

NavPress is the publishing ministry of The Navigators. The mission of NavPress is to reach, disciple, and equip people to know Christ and make Him known by publishing life-related materials that are biblically rooted and culturally relevant. Our vision is to stimulate spiritual transformation through every product we publish.

© 2007 by John Shore

NAVPRESS, BRINGING TRUTH TO LIFE, and the NAVPRESS logo are registered trademarks of NavPress. Absence of ® in connection with marks of NavPress or other parties does not indicate an absence of registration of those marks.

ISBN 1-60006-057-9
ISBN 9-78160006-057-1

Cover design by Wes Youssi / The Designworks Group www.thedesignworksgroup.com.
Cover image by Getty Images
Creative Team: Jeff Gerke, Traci Mullins, Darla Hightower, Arvid Wallen, Kathy Guist

Some of the anecdotal illustrations in this book are true to life and are included with the permission of the persons involved. All other illustrations are composites of real situations, and any resemblance to people living or dead is coincidental.

Unless otherwise identified, all Scripture quotations in this publication are taken from the HOLY BIBLE: NEW INTERNATIONAL VERSION® (NIV®). Copyright © 1973, 1978, 1984 by International Bible Society. Used by permission of Zondervan Publishing House. All rights reserved.

Library of Congress Cataloging-in-Publication Data
Shore, John, 1958-
 I'm OK, you're not : the message we're sending unbelievers and why we should stop / by John Shore.
  p. cm.
 ISBN 1-60006-057-9
 1. Witness bearing (Christianity) 2. Evangelistic work. 3. Christian life. I. Title.
BV4520.S46 2007
269'.2--dc22
                                  2006029647

Printed in the United States of America

1 2 3 4 5 6 7 8 / 11 10 09 08 07

Dedication

To my wife Cat, whose love never, ever fails

The commandments, "Do not commit adultery," "Do not murder," "Do not steal," "Do not covet," and whatever other commandment there may be, are summed up in this one rule: "Love your neighbor as yourself." Romans 13:9

So in everything, do to others what you would have them do to you, for this sums up the Law and the Prophets. Matthew 7:12

Contents

Induction – I Mean. Introduction

INDUCTION. THAT'S SO . . . TOTALLY not it. Sorry.

Although that that's *not* it pretty much *is* the entire point of this book.

But. First things first.

And the first thing that comes to my mind whenever I think of the words "book introduction" is, "Now I'm so bored I need to die." So let me keep this book introduction short.

Reader, book.

Book, reader.

John Shore
San Diego, 2007

Har! *That,* my friends, is the kind of Major Humor you can expect from this here tome!

Whoo-hoo! Party on, Reader Dudes!

Wait! Wait! Come back!

I'm sorry: What I *meant* to say is that there will be absolutely no more humor in this book. My sole reason for getting that little bit of it out of the way right up front was so that we'd then be free to concentrate. And what I'm suggesting we concentrate *upon* is this book's Core Idea, which is that here in America we (loving, lovely) Christians have for so long now been so energetically endeavoring to fulfill the Great Commission that it's reasonable to wonder whether or not at this point we are, by continuing to press upon people a belief system they already know about and have already rejected, working not only to the detriment of the Great Commission, but also against that *other* humongous To Do item Jesus gave us — the Great Commandment.

I mean, I'm totally just an Average Layperson, for sure — but I'm pretty sure that's all anyone needs to be in order to at least know that Christ gave his followers two Colossal Directives: the Great Commission and the Great Commandment, right? The former, of course, tells us (in so many words) to do our best to try to convert nonbelievers into Christians ("Therefore go and make disciples of all nations . . . teaching them to obey everything I have commanded you."); the latter (after "Love the Lord your God with all your heart") enjoins us to "Love your neighbor as yourself."

So, as far as I can tell, the two Big Messages of our Lord, taken together, amount to, "Love everyone, Christian or not — but if they're *not* Christian, do what you can to change that."

In other words, love non-Christians — but desire that they change.

Um.

If someone said to you, "I love you — but I want you to change the very essence of who you are," would you feel all warm and fuzzy inside, or . . . not exactly?

As you may know, *I Love You, You're Perfect, Now Change* is the name of a very popular modern stage musical. I've seen it. It's pretty funny!

And that *title!* Automatically funny!

Except for, you know, how it's also kind of not.

The problem is that with his Great Commandment, Jesus didn't direct us to love our neighbors once they become Christians, or get their lives together, or lend us money, or tell us how much they like our new haircuts. And he certainly didn't tell us that it was okay for us to *stop* loving a person after they'd chosen not to become Christian. No—all of that would make it much too easy for us. God's (self-proclaimed) supreme directive to us is as unequivocal as a lightning bolt to the heart. He told us to love our neighbors as we love ourselves—period, end of story, that's it.

Which still leaves us with the Genuine Conundrum of trying to figure out how exactly to love someone like the Great Commandment says to, *and* to at the same time desire that they change, as the Great Commission indicates we must. It's like saying, "I absolutely, utterly, and without qualification love that painting; I wish it was a sea anemone." How can both be true? How can you really love what something *is,* and at the same time desire it to be something other than what it is? Isn't it true that if it's our profound desire that any given nonbeliever change (and especially if we want them to undergo a transformation as radical as the one from non-Christian to Christian), then the *best* we can do is love the *idea* of who we think they would be if they became someone radically different from the person they are? (And thus do I prove that everyday, normal people can be just as confusing as Brainy Theologians.) But we cannot truly *love* the nonbeliever as they are when we find them, because love (that is, love between two mature adults) comprises not only genuine affection, but also respect and acceptance.

What's certainly true—and what certainly deserves celebration—is the degree to which we Christians have, in fact, always Harkened Mightily to the call of the Great Commission. So winning, in fact, have been their/our efforts in that noble enterprise that just about the only people in America today who *don't* know a fair amount about Jesus — who don't at least know that he was God on earth, performed miracles, sacrificed himself to atone for our sins, and rose from the dead — are people who have never known more than, say, ten other people — and who also don't have a TV, never listen to the radio, never read, and never go to the movies.

Which amounts to just about no one at all.

Yay! Pretty much every last, single person in America has heard the word of God! The Great Commission has gone a very long way toward being completely fulfilled right here in our own backyard!

Whoo-hoo!

We rock!

Well done, good and faithful servants!

Glory be to God!

So. Now what?

Well, the contention of this book is that now that it's safe to assume that all of our neighbors already know the story of Christ and the Bible and so on, it might be a good time to take some of that enormous energy we currently spend on converting those same people, and to focus it instead on "just" loving them as much as we love ourselves.

In other words, I think that here in the great, gospel-saturated U.S. of A., it's time to shift our concentration from fulfilling the Great Commission to fulfilling the Great Commandment.

I do want to be clear about the caveat, though, of "only" meaning that we should ease off trying to tell people about Christ who haven't first *asked* us to tell them about Christ. If someone has indicated to us that they're open to hearing the Good News, then by all means let us share until we're hoarse (or until it's clear they'd like us to go home so that they can go to bed). By extension, then, I'm also not in any way meaning to suggest that preachers should stop preaching, or that stadium-filling Billy Graham-style revival meetings should stop happening. Of course they shouldn't. Because again: Those kinds of public or corporate affairs are presented to people who have *asked* to participate in them, who have willingly volunteered to hear the Word of God. Such people are fair game — and have at 'em then, I say! Praise the Lord, and save me a front row seat.

So you see what I'm saying: If someone, of their own accord, has opened the door to Christ, of course it's our treasured obligation to usher the Lord right on in (and to then quickly step aside, and try not to talk too much). But if the person we'd like to convert *hasn't* opened that door themselves, then we need to stop huffing, and puffing, and trying to blow their door down anyway.

Because what I think is now officially Working Against Us All is that entirely too-common dynamic wherein a Christian and a non-Christian get together, and neither of them can *relax* at all, because the Christian is always (at whatever level) wondering how he can convert the non-Christian, and the non-Christian is always (at whatever level) dreading the inevitable moment when the Christian starts trying to do that very thing.

Back before I was a Christian, whenever I had a conversation with a Christian I was always just *waiting* for the moment they'd start trying to convert me. And that moment inevitably arrived. Sometimes the attempt was subtle ("So, do you go to any kind of church, or anything?"); sometimes it was overt ("So, have you heard the word of the Lord?"); sometimes it was just plain scary ("So, do you know you need to repent of your sins and accept Jesus as your personal savior if you don't want to spend all of eternity burning in hell?"). But always, it arrived.

Not particularly good for the Great Commission — and not

doing a lot for the Great Commandment, either. It's not good for the Great Commission because it simply doesn't work: A person on the receiving end of the message that in order to become a better (or at least "okay") person they need undergo a radical transformation is generally inspired to do nothing so much as hightail it away from the messenger. And it's not good for the Great Commandment, either, since once an evangelizer and his or her would-be Christian have split up, their relationship is finished—and unless the Hallmark company has come up with some truly amazing new card I haven't yet heard about, it's just not possible to love someone with whom you have no relationship at all.

The bottom line is that no matter how artfully we put it, or how passionately or sincerely we mean them well, when we convey to an unbeliever the message that they really *need* to become Christian, the only thing they can possibly understand us to be saying—the only thing *we'd* hear if we were in their shoes—is that we're okay, and that they most definitely are not.

We're great; they're on their way to perdition.

A message not exactly cockle-warming to hear. Which is why unbelievers, as we all know, never listen to it for very long at all.

Besides, doesn't a Great Commandment totally trump a Great Commission? Isn't it a much bigger deal to be *commanded* to do something than it is to be *commissioned* to do it? If you arrived at your office one day to find five grim, strapping guys in dark suits waiting for you, and one of them stepped forward and said, "We are from the government of the United States of America, and you have been officially commissioned to do something for us," you'd be mighty impressed, for sure. But if that same guy said, "We are from the government of the United States of America, and you have been officially commanded to do something for us," you'd have a heart attack.

The first statement was pretty darn dramatic. The second . . . well, killed you.

The point is: Just on the *face* of it, shouldn't we pay a lot more attention to fulfilling the Great Commandment than we do to fulfilling the Great Commission? (Yes. I'm submitting that the answer is "Yes.")

And let us, by the by, not forget that Jesus himself never referred to what he said in Matthew 28 as the "Great Commission"—that those are *our words,* not his. (Isn't that weird? Didn't you always assume that somewhere in the Bible Jesus *did* say something like, "Forget not what I tell you, my faithful followers, for this is the Great Commission," or, "Now harken up, my hearty disciples, for verily am I about to reveal unto you that which, if I have anything to say about it, will henceforth and forever be known as the Great Commission"? Didn't you think that? Oh. Well, I did. But I was wrong. Jesus, as it turns out, no more ever used the words "Great Commission" than he did, "You're not my real father!" or "Toga party!")

One thing seems certain enough: This whole intra-America, Christian vs. non-Christian nonsense we all live with every day has got to stop. It's like our whole red-and-blue country has become L.A.-style gang territory, with Bloods on one side, and Crips on the other. (With Christians, of course, being the Bloods—and with blue being the color of the non-believing Crips, who are blue because somewhere deep inside them they know they're going to hell. Oh, wait! Sorry! *Bad Christian!*)

The bottom line is that believers and nonbelievers need to move as close spiritually, intellectually, and psychologically as they are physically. (And while that's really *close,* of course, it's not, you know, occupying-the-same-*space* close. I mean, let's not get carried away.) Doing whatever we can to help make that happen is not only the right thing to do morally and socially, it's the right thing to do biblically. We can't love our neighbors—that is, we can't fulfill the Great Commandment—if we barely *know* our neighbors. And it's a sure bet that those who from here on out I'll often refer to as Normies—that is, typical, everyday people who (though they may consider themselves "spiritual") don't ascribe to any particular religion—aren't going to spend a lot of time wondering how they can adjust the state of their minds and souls in order to get closer to we religious types. Building that bridge is something we're going to have to do.

It's something Jesus explicitly *commanded* us to do.

So . . . we should, then.

Yours in the mind-bogglingly beneficent grace of our Lord,

John

FOR THE SAKE OF FOCUS and brevity, this book assumes that Christians hold the Great Commission as their primary, overriding motivator to evangelize. But there are of course other passages in the Bible that also encourage us to evangelize. At the end of this book (under "More Heart, Really, Than Appendix"), I have collected some of the most commonly cited of those passages; each is followed by a brief comment or two explaining why I can't understand it either, as meaning that all of us Christians in America today need to get out there and buy a bullhorn, exactly.

Also, in the course of preparing this book I turned for help to www.craigslist.org. (Most big cities in America have their own Craigslist site; they're unadorned, free, community-based sites where people look for jobs, or post stuff they have for sale, or try to find activity partners, and so on.) In various cities, under "writing gigs," I posted that I was looking for short statements from any non-Christian who thought they might have anything whatsoever to say to Christians. I was careful to word the notice in a manner so utterly bland and non-committal that I was pretty sure no one would respond to it at all. But I thought that if anyone did, it might provide for some interesting commentary for the book.

Well, they did—and it did. You will find the responses I received, placed in no particular order just before the discussion questions at the end of each chapter (under "Ouch"). I of course don't necessarily agree with these statements—some of them are painfully harsh toward us. But I put them in the book anyway, because I thought they might shed some light on how some Normies, sometimes, see us. In the course of collecting these testimonies I naturally ended up exchanging a few e-mails back and forth with each of their writers, every one of whom came across as thoughtful and good-natured. The majority of them also struck me as being mostly *sad* about the current state of the general relationship in this country between Christians and non-Christians. That really surprised me. Where I expected mostly anger, I got instead a kind of pervasive, resigned bewilderment.

If you boiled down to one thought the overall sentiment most often expressed in the nonbelievers' collective statements, it'd be, "Why do Christians hate us so?" Which, of course, was a deeply painful thing to read in so many different ways, from so many different people.

1

Oh, Say Can We Seeeeee Them?

WHETHER YOU'RE A CHRISTIAN or not (and, let's face it, if you're reading this book you probably are), you're already familiar with the Great Divide that exists in this country between Christians and Normies. (In case you skipped the introduction, by "Normies," I mean regular, everyday people who haven't exactly spent so much of their lives praying that now their knees are shot. Book intros and God: First Things that are totally necessary, yet tempting to ignore because they so often seem too somber and imposing to be actually engaging. Really makes you think, doesn't it? *Now get back there, Skippy, and read that intro!*) On one side of our national cultural divide are the non-believing Normies, dancing and smoking and engaging in all kinds of behaviors we Christians wouldn't be caught dead even *thinking* about in the middle of the night when we're wide awake and everyone else is asleep and our computer's just sitting there like a golden ticket to Secret Shimmering Excitement Land—and we Christians are here on the other side, trying to please God. (And constantly failing at it, of course, and then feeling guilty about that, and then—praise the Lord!—turning back to God, and availing ourselves of his boundless grace and mercy, and then . . . well . . . you know the routine.)

And the two sides—We Christians and Those Normies— pretty much stay in their own camps.

As (I think) the great Robert Frost so elegantly put it: "East is East and West is West / And everyone likes their own kind best" (from Frost's classic, "People: I'd Trade 'Em All for a Decent Bowl of Oatmeal").

Poetry is so beautiful.

It seems obvious enough that the primary reason Christians and Normies tend to stay so isolated from each other is because it's just so much easier and rewarding to talk to someone with whom you share a whole host (so to speak) of core values. If you're a Christian, you know how it sometimes feels as if you couldn't get a decent conversation going with a Normie if the two of you were being held captive on an alien spaceship. It's like you could have both experienced totally rude Martian Probing—and you *still* wouldn't have all that much in common. You'd both be standing upright, your arms tied behind you around gleaming silver Spaceship Poles, and your conversation would only amount to something along the lines of:

> YOU: Boy. Just wait'll my pastor back home hears about *this*.
> NORMIE: I'll bet.
> YOU: He and I are *definitely* going to have to go back over the book of Genesis together, I can tell you that.
> NORMIE: Oh. Sure.
> YOU: Don't recall any space aliens in there.
> NORMIE: Guess not.
> YOU: I mean, you always hear about Martians being crazy and obnoxious, but until you actually *experience* it, you really have no idea.
> NORMIE: That's true.
> YOU: You must be completely freaked. I know I am.
> NORMIE: I'm pretty hungry, actually. I could really go for a double cheeseburger.

YOU: Really? You're *hungry?*

NORMIE: Yeah.

YOU: Well, I guess you're in luck, then—what are the chances that they *don't* have a McDonald's on whatever planet they're taking us to? Ha, ha. [Long pause] I was coming home from my Bible study group when the aliens got me. How 'bout you?

NORMIE: I was at home watching TV.

YOU: Wow. That's really awful.

NORMIE: Yeah.

YOU: You must have been terrified.

NORMIE: It was pretty scary, that's for sure.

YOU [Long pause]: What were you watching?

NORMIE: *Friends.* That's such a great show. I thought that thing with Rachel and Ross got a little boring, though.

YOU [Long pause]: I've never really seen that show.

NORMIE: Oh.

YOU [Long pause]: I've heard it's great, though.

NORMIE: Yeah. It is.

YOU: It's pretty funny, right?

NORMIE: Right.

YOU [Long pause]: Funny's good.

NORMIE: Funny's great.

YOU: Yeah.

NORMIE: Yep.

See? Flat as Terrible Movie dialogue. Because in order for any two people—much less any two strangers—to really click, they've got to share something in common significantly more profound than working in the same place, or living in the same neighborhood, or even being held captive together on the same alien spaceship.

Which is precisely why whenever you put just about any two Christians together, they start clicking like a Geiger Counter at a leaky nuclear power plant.

As an example of the Clicking Christian phenomenon, I recall the time, about two weeks after I converted, when right after a Sunday service, a fellow believer to whom I was being introduced stuck out his hand, and with Maximum Good Cheer said to me, "So you're the guy who had the sudden conversion in the supply closet at his job, right?"

"Right," I said, shaking his hand. "That did happen to me."

"And that was, what, about two weeks ago? Amazing! Praise the Lord! So, has your whole life turned to [expletive deleted, because you can't *in any way* curse in a book intended for a Christian audience] yet?"

As I continued smiling, I thought: "Wow, this guy is *so* going to hell for bellowing out [expletive deleted] right here in church. I better back away; he might just spontaneously combust." No — what I really thought was, "Wow! What a great conversation this already is!" (What my new friend was referring to, of course, was how the Lord, once he decides to insist it belongs to him, can totally ravage your life. As any adult Sudden Convert knows, in some ways being born again can be almost as [non-biologically] messy as being born the first time.)

"You wouldn't believe what happened to me after *I* converted!" continued Joe Jovial. "Within a month of finding the Lord, I'd lost my job, and my girlfriend — *and* I was diagnosed with Hodgkin's Disease! Turns out I had *cancer!*" He looked positively ecstatic. "Isn't that *unbelievable?!*"

"Wow," I said. "It really is."

Then he told me how he "beat the crap" out of his cancer — and we went on, right there in the middle of our church's packed lobby, to have the most wonderful conversation about God, physical pain, relationship pain, and pretty much Everything That Counts.

And after we'd shaken hands again and agreed to have lunch together sometime, I thought: "So. That's how Christians who don't even *know* each other relate to each other!"

Bounding down the stairs away from the church, I thought: "Sweet! Bring me more Christians!"

It felt so great, belonging to a club in which everyone shared the same profoundly important beliefs—and were so often so refreshingly open about what those beliefs really *meant* to them.

I come from a family where you couldn't get a decent conversation going about anything real if someone barfed up the Holy Grail right in the middle of dinner.

This was better!

Of course, in The Very Best World Ever (or in at least one version of it), *everyone* would be Christian. How cool would that be? How great would it be if you could just walk down the street, and cry out, "I'm feelin' God's love!" without getting instantly mugged by offended strangers? Driving by your neighbors, you'd be able to roll down your window and call to them, "Hallelujah!" without later worrying you'd forced them to sell their house and move to Tibet. You'd be able to say on a city bus, "C'mon, everybody! Let's pray and thank the Lord!" without . . . well . . . being reminded that municipal buses and spontaneous exclamations about God are One Bad Combo.

In that fabulous, all-Christian world you'd be able to, say, hang around the company water cooler at your job, and instead of talking with your coworkers about the movie you saw the weekend before, or how it seems to rain every single time you wash your car, or about some other thing you kind of care about but that wouldn't exactly overwhelm you on your deathbed, you'd instead talk with them about what sins you've lately been burdened with, and what you're going to do about getting yourself right with God again, and about how grateful you are that no matter how far you stray from the love of the Lord, he's always right there, patiently and lovingly waiting for you to renounce evil, turn around, and come back home.

And they would hug you.

And they would pray for you.

And all of you would feel in your hearts the boundless, shining mercy of God, whose presence you would sense amongst you as surely as you'd hear the water gurgling in the bottle beside you.

Go ahead.

Dare to dream it.

Dare to imagine a world in which everyone is a brother or sister in Christ.

Ahhhhhh.

Feel the love.

Okay, that's enough. You can stop dreaming about that now.

I say: You can stop dreaming about that.

C'mon, now. I'm serious. That's enough.

Stop dreaming about a world where everyone's a Christian!

And do you know why you (and I) need to stop dreaming about a world in which everyone is Christian? Because we're human. And a really big part of being human is trying to get what we want. And if we want a world wherein everyone's a Christian, then that's going to trigger our desire to fulfill the Great Commission.

And that means that we're going to go out there, and start witnessing, or evangelizing, or proselytizing, or doing *something* to try to change someone who isn't a Christian into one.

And *that*, I'm afraid, is when we're going to be in very grave danger of becoming exactly the sort of Christian who (alas) is so often seen by Normies as being little if anything but pushy, dogmatic, and alienating.

Again (and again and again): I would be the last person on the planet to deny the absolute importance of delivering the Good News to people who have either requested it or never gotten it at all. If someone hasn't yet heard of Jesus Christ, it's imperative that we who believe make sure they *do* hear that word. No Christian in the world would even think about questioning that.

It's the *"hasn't yet heard of Jesus Christ"* part that I think at this point in the history of our faith deserves our attention. I'm convinced that these days one of the most important things we need to bear in mind about the Great Commission is its historical context. I just don't see any way around how critical it is for us to remember that when Christ directed his disciples to get out there and spread his message, almost no one in the world had even *heard* of him yet. The story of God's coming to earth as a man had happened so recently that it was . . . well, still happening. Then it *was* a Great Commission—then it was the commission to beat all commissions, and no doubt about it. Once the first disciples received their famous marching orders, it was Beyond Important that they get right out there, start knocking on strangers' doors, and start saying to whomever answered something like:

"Hello there. You don't know me—and please excuse me, right now, for how weird I know this is going to sound—but, well, you know how these days a lot of people believe in just one God—in one huge, all-powerful Super Entity, who exists up in the heavens somewhere, and who sees and knows everything that ever happens anywhere in the world? You're familiar with that concept, right? Okay, well—and again, I know somewhere in here you're bound to start thinking that I'm making a bid for the position of Village

Idiot, but if you could just bear with me — it turns out there *is* just one God! And what happened, see, is that that God became a *man!* Yeah, a regular man, just like ... well, not *just* like any other man, but close enough. And this God-man came down to earth, see, and he performed all these miracles — healing people, driving demons away, raising people from the dead, even — and then, right outside of Jerusalem, he was *crucified* by Roman soldiers!

"No, I'm not kidding. It really happened! It was horrible. You honestly didn't hear anything about it? You probably noticed when it actually *affected the weather*, though, didn't you? Again, with the am I kidding — *no,* I'm not kidding! Does this sound like the kind of thing a person would joke about? Didn't you notice at around noon on — well, gosh, I guess it's already four weeks ago this Friday — when all of a sudden the whole *sky* turned dark? Didn't you see that?

"You didn't? What, are *you* kidding? How could you have missed something like that? Oh, I see you don't have any windows in your hut. Then you *must* have been inside at the moment of this terrible and wondrous event, because it wasn't something you could miss. *Everyone* went berserk over it. Dark as night, in the middle of the day! One minute it's hot, you're sweating, you're casting a shadow — and the next, boom! — you can't see your hand in front of your face. Truly amazing. Surely you read *something* about it in *The Weekly Tablet?* No? That's odd; they did a whole top-of-the-slab story on it. Well, no, I don't know if it was *the* headline story or not — probably not, now that I think of it, since that was the week the Jerusalem Wild Donkeys finally beat the Amman Giants in the All-Palestine Olympics. But believe me, everyone was talking about what happened. And I have a feeling everyone's *going* to be talking about it for a very long time to come. Interested in hearing more about it yourself? Sure, we can talk while you pulverize dates. My own mother was a top-notch pulverizer of dates—but my father married her anyway!"

So, let's see . . . that would be one of the lesser known disciples, Chatticus.

No, but of course at the dawn of Christianity it was essential for everyone In The Know to get out there, and do everything they could to make sure people everywhere heard the brand-new news. That simply had to happen. If it hadn't, then today we'd all probably be worshiping the wheel, or yeast, or something. Proselytizing was vital when Paul was doing (the heck!) out of it; it was vital when the Goths and Vandals were . . . I don't know . . . throwing rocks at and Generally Hassling all the indentured serfs who were just trying to get a little shut-eye before their next big day on the mud farm; it was something we might have expected Buzz Aldrin to do if he, Neil Armstrong, and . . . that other guy . . . had come across anyone on the moon.

And it goes without saying that we Christians all hope and pray that someday the moon is how far away we'll have to go in order to find someone who has yet to hear the story of Jesus. In an effort to realize that dream, legions of loving, intrepid Christians are currently doing us all proud by delivering the Good News to every last corner of the world. Praise be to those brave hearts! And we here at home are certainly doing our part to support those good Christian workers. As far as I know, just about every church in America helps support some missionary, somewhere.

Not too long after becoming a Christian I got a job with a Rescue Mission as Guy Who Goes Around To Churches And Tells Them About The Rescue Mission So They'll Donate Money To It. In that capacity I visited a lot of churches, and met with a lot of (the very nicest!) missionary committee members. And being so new to the faith I was just amazed to discover how every single church I visited had or was supporting someone, somewhere: In Central America, South America, Africa, Russia, China, the Middle East, Des Moines ... everywhere. Hanging up inside the sanctuary of one megachurch I visited were giant, parade-worthy flags from every country in which its congregants had stationed missionaries. It was like being inside the United Nations building. I recognized maybe two of the flags. I drove the poor woman beside me on the pew crazy.

"Where's that one from?" I whispered, pointing to one of the flags. "The green one there, with the black triangles."

She looked up at the flag, and then back at me. "Ghaznia," she whispered. (Or something like that; I couldn't quite make her out.)

"What about the one next to it, with the red circles?" I whispered.

"Hyppnondia."

"How about that bright yellow one over there?"

"Zuchnia."

"What about ..."

"I'm sorry, but do you mind? This isn't *The Travel Channel*. It's church. I'm trying to hear the pastor."

She was right, of course: We were at church. So of course I did the right thing: I apologized to her, faced front—and then, right after the very next hymn, "accidentally" sat down on her program.

Anyway, it's wonderful the way we're carrying to the remotest parts of the world the story that means so very much to us. But what for our purposes here is important to bear in mind is that in America today there are very few, if any, places where the story of Jesus hasn't already penetrated, but deeply. Christianity is so integral to the history and culture of our country that there'd have to be something truly unique about a person's upbringing and/or life for them to have grown up in or spent any real time in America and not at least know who Jesus was, what his relationship was to God, and why Christians believe in him as we do.

The practical fact is that if we go out to evangelize in Anytown, USA, we're pretty much guaranteed to run into one of two kinds of (grown-up) people: those who are already Christian, and those who have already decided that they don't want to be Christian.

And of course it's the latter group with whom I think we'd do well to consider changing both the motivation for and substance of our interactions, because they've already decided that Christianity isn't their cup of tea. Using their God-given minds and free will, these rational, sane, fully functional people have concluded that the overall good of their hearts and souls is best served in a way that's different from the way we believe God nurtures ours.

Not to be too Johnny One Note or anything, but for us to continue to convey to someone who is consciously aware that they don't want something the message that, in fact, they *do* want that thing but just haven't yet realized it, can only create a dynamic wherein the person we're trying to "help" pretty instantly becomes extremely clear about one thing, anyway, which is that they don't want to be around *us* anymore at all.

And then, as soon as they possibly can, they leave us.

And then we're left alone, clutching our Bible, wondering if there was some other way we could have more effectively communicated our message, something else we might have said that wouldn't have turned them off.

But there is no such thing.

And there won't ever be such a thing.

And that's a fact that I'm thinking it's time we just acknowledged.

Ouch

"I am often distressed at the way some Christians take as a given that Christians and Christianity define goodness. Many of we non-Christians make a practice of doing good; we, too, have a well-developed ethical system, and are devoted to making the world a better place. Christians hardly have a monopoly on what's right, or good, or just."—C.R., SEATTLE

"I feel that Christians have got it all wrong; it seems to me that they've created the very thing Jesus was against: Separatism."
—T. O., DENVER

"Many of the 'God fearing' Christians I've met over the years who have tried to convince me to attend their church and stop living a sinner's life were among the most immoral people I've ever met. Whatever happened to 'Thou shall not judge'? I live a good life. I'm a firm believer in karma, and am therefore very thoughtful of my actions and words. I strive to cause no harm to any person or animal. I have raised my children to respect their elders; to say please, thank you, and excuse me; to hold the door for others, etc. I am often told what wonderfully polite and respectful children I have. I am happily married, and would never cheat on my husband. I do not lie; I do not steal; I would never dream of causing ill will to anyone—and yet, to a Christian, I am nothing more than a sinner condemned to hell. It is that very narrow-mindedness that has driven me far from Christianity. To make matters worse, often the very people who try to persuade me to convert to Christianity lie, backstab, have adulterous affairs, have unruly children, and are the first to start kicking someone when they're down. I am now a Buddhist, and for that I thank every Christian I have ever met."
—H. W., PHOENIX

"Quite frankly, I get annoyed when evangelicals approach me. They somehow think they have an inside track on all things spiritual and that their version of reality is the only one. For an evangelical Christian to try to tell me that his and only his faith is the one true faith is either the height of arrogance or the depth of ignorance. Everyone has the right to believe whatever he or she finds comforting to believe, but no one has the right to try to force their beliefs on others."—B. P., KANSAS CITY, MO

"Christians seem to have lost their focus on Jesus' core message: 'Love the Lord your God with all your heart and with all your soul, and love your neighbor as you love yourself.'"—R. M., TACOMA, WA

Talk Amongst Yourselves

How real do you think the "Great Divide" is between Christians and Normies in America? What's been your personal experience trying to bridge that divide?

Do you prefer the company of Christians to that of Normies? Why or why not?

What do you think (or know) that it's like being inside the mind of a person who doesn't ascribe to any particular religion at all? If you've always been Christian, do you think you can even begin to guess what it's like to be a Normie?

Are there any ways in which you think the world might *not* be a better place if everyone in it were Christian?

Do you think there's any chance that that woman believed that I sat on her bulletin by accident?

2

How Dare They Leave
When We're Offending Them

THE PROBLEM WITH OUR in any way communicating to a nonbeliever that they really should be Christian is that, no matter how we put it, what we're really saying is that they need to change. And no one—no Christian, Muslim, Jewish person, French girl, Chinese guy, mermaid—*no one* likes to be told what they should do. You suggest to a guy who just burst into flames that he should run and jump into the lake that's ten feet to his left, and chances are he'll move two feet to his right, and claim that what he was *really* hoping for was someone to come along with a bag of marshmallows and a stick. That's how people are. We all just *hate* being told what to do.

I sure do, anyway—and unless I suddenly grow flippers or something, I'm about as typical a person as you could find. And I *know* as a kid I drove my poor father crazy. I remember him standing in my bedroom when I was about twelve, exasperatedly crying, "What *is* it with you, anyway? I swear, the only way I could get you to clean up this room would be to tell you *not* to. *Then* you'd attack this mess like there was gold hidden under it somewhere. You drive me insane with your stubbornness. I'll tell you what: *Don't* empty the garbage after dinner tonight. *Don't* weed the side yard this weekend. And by all means, I *command* you not to get A's on any of your school tests!"

My dad. He was such a . . . taller version of Don Rickles. And while I learned a great deal from his humor and near-desperate implorations, what I always found especially endearing was the tenacity with which he clung to the idea that I would ever respond to his telling me what to do in precisely the manner he hoped.

Poor guy. If only he hadn't had . . . well, me.

But he did have me. And I, being human, was forever chafing against being told what to do. And what I think we need to be aware of is that, as evangelizing Christians, we aren't (however subtly) just telling people what to *do*, either. It's not like we're Safety Monitors telling Normies not to run in the hallway, or supervisors trying to get Normies to correctly fill out their time cards. No — we're taking Making Helpful Suggestions to a whoooooooole other level. When we try to convert a Normie, we're telling that person what they should actually *be*. We're jamming our fingers (and, let's face it, sticking our noses) into the very core of who they are, and going, "What the heck is *this?* How long has this over *here* been here? And what in the Sam Hill is going on with this whole area over *here?* Just *look* at this place! What a mess!"

See? Again with the cold cockles. Can we really *blame* Normies for sometimes ducking the other way when they see us coming? You tell a person that they need to change — *especially* that they need to change the very essence of who they are — and the harsh fact of the matter is that you just called them a loser. Or, at least, it's perfectly reasonable for us to expect that that's exactly what any sane, rational, adult Normie is going to hear every time one of us tells them that for their own good they need to believe in Jesus the way we do. How thrilled would any of *us* be if someone tried to convince us that we were, say, doomed to an eternity of damnation if we didn't pledge our lives to Allah, or Buddha, or Ganesh? The second we heard that, we'd think four things about the person saying it to us: 1. They're wrong; 2. They're crazy; 3. They're arrogant; and 4. They're insufferably rude.

Which is why that's such a weird, ineffective way for any of us to try to open up anyone else's heart to what we have to say.

And why it soooooo doesn't work. And let's face it: We can say what we like about winning converts to Christianity in America, but the one thing we're *stuck* saying about it is that it isn't, exactly, to anything near an overwhelming degree, working.

And I can prove it, too, man.

Though I'm sure my little Personal Anecdote about my dad is all the proof you require.

How's that, now? It's *not*, you say?

Wow. Tough crowd. And here I thought we Christians were all about supporting one another.

Okay, fine. *Fine.*

Be that way.

Looks like it's time for me to Bust Out The Facts.

The 2004 General Social Survey, done by the University of Chicago's National Opinion Research Center (hey! wake up! I'm bustin' out the facts!), showed that between 1993 and 2002 the share of Americans who said they were Protestant dropped from 63 to 52 percent. The calculator-wielding brainiacs who did this study (which was based on over thirty years of religious identification studies) were very comfortable asserting that, by the end of 2006, for the first time in America's history, Protestants would be less than half the population. (Wait. This book'll be published by then! Well? Was the University of Chicago right? Are less than half of us now Protestants? If not, yay! If so, then . . . let's all work out a secret code that lets us communicate unbeknownst to our new Normie Overlords. And we will bow our heads, and meekly do the bidding of our pagan masters, and silently gather our strength until the day of our uprising when in an overwhelming display of strength and courage *we take back from the Evil Ones the glorious reigns of power which once belonged to us!* Uh. Right. So I need to cut down on the coffee.)

An article about the U of C study, published in the July 21, 2004, issue of *The Houston Chronicle* (titled, unsurprisingly, *"Study finds number of Protestants is falling"*) summed up The Big Picture this way: "Mainline Protestant denominations have been hemorrhaging members for decades."

Another source to which people often turn for hard data about religion in America is (okay: now's the time to take that hefty cappuccino sip) The Graduate Center of the City University of New York's American Religious Identification Survey (ARIS). This 2001 mondo-study essentially served as a follow-up to the center's 1990 National Survey of Religious Identification (NSRI). Taken together, these studies unequivocally demonstrated that sociologists have *got* to start coming up with catchier names for their studies.

No—but what the ARIS study found (amongst massive amounts of other stuff) is that almost 30 million Americans are not affiliated with any organized religion—a number that in the proceeding ten years had more than *doubled*—and that is greater than all of our country's Methodists, Lutherans, and Episcopalians combined. The report also found (get this!) that the fastest growing religion in America is Wicca—the belief system adhered to by devout witches (which—surprise!—come in both female and male) everywhere. In 1990, there were amongst us about 8,000 Wiccans (Wiccaneos? Wiccastians? Wicci?); in 2001, 134,000 of our fellow citizens were proud to call themselves witches. And, according to that 2001 ARIS study, the number of Wicci in this country is *doubling about every thirty months.*

Hide your giant cauldrons!

Weigh down your monkeys!

Resist the temptation to invest in Brooms, Inc.!

The guy to whom a *lot* of leading Christians turn for information on the state of American Christianity is George Barna, who runs an organization in southern California called (you guessed it) The Barna Group, a marketing research company that regularly pumps out detailed reports on seemingly every facet of the practice of modern Christianity in America. Mr. Barna and his reports are renowned for periodically causing church leaders across the country to break out into hives.

He's also known for the quality of his polling data. (In a cover story about him published in the summer of 2002, *Christianity Today* said that Mr. Barna "is to evangelicals what George Gallup is to the larger culture.") In January of every year since 1991, Mr. Barna's company issues its State of the Church survey; it then follows that report with documents essentially summing up or exploring particular aspects of that year's collected data. Pretty nifty!

Here was how Mr. Barna summed up his 2001 State of the Church survey: "America certainly did not experience the spiritual revival that many Christians hoped would emerge as the new millennium began. In fact, Americans seem to have become almost inoculated to spiritual events, outreach efforts, and the quest for personal spiritual development. There are magnificent exceptions throughout the country, but overall, Christian ministry is in a deep rut."

A salient point to emerge from his latest report as of this writing (*State of the Church: 2005*) is that one-third (34 percent) of all adults are unchurched—a proportion that has changed little over the past five years. (And you know how New Englanders are supposed to be Intensely Independent? Well, apparently they really are: 42 percent of adults in the Northeast aren't involved with any church at all.)

Mr. Barna's latest report also shows that evangelicals remain just 7 percent of the adult population—a percentage that hasn't changed since his company started tracking such matters in 1994.

So. There it is: It's just not really happening for us. And let's face it: It's not like we need a pie chart to prove it to us, either.

We know it.

We know that about the same number of people show up to our church every single Sunday morning. (Unless, that is, we worship at a megachurch. And then who knows *what* the heck is going on on the other side of our six-acre Hallelujah Hippodrome, where they seem to be listening to a whole other *concert* than we are.)

We know how rarely we see a new face in our Bible study class.

We know that every Sunday at our church we put out the same number of donuts (or less!) that we've been putting out ever since we first started gaining Church Poundage.

Though I suppose at some of our churches we're putting out truffles, or caviar, or handing out platinum-plated hand fans, or giving away free gold teeth, or *something*, because, as Mr. Barna told *Christianity Today* in that cover story about him, every year, American churches spend fifty to sixty billion dollars on domestic ministry.

That's fifty to sixty *billion* dollars. To help you gain perspective on how much money that really is, imagine for a moment that you have one dollar in the pocket of your pants. Now imagine adding to that dollar 59,999,999,999 other dollars. Think how full your pants would be! You'd have to *roll* everywhere you went. No—it'd be worse: You wouldn't be able to move at all. If people wanted to visit with you, they'd have to fly up to your head in a blimp.

Think of it, man: *Only* blimp-based relationships.

That's just a lot of money. It's so much, in fact, that I think from now on all of us can feel perfectly within our rights to demand that, instead of regular donuts between our church's services, we get éclairs. That have been kept ever so slightly chilled. By the Team Éclair we now staff full-time.

All that money, and we're *still* losing people.

The Bible *does* tell believers to evangelize; there's no question about that. But even if we disregard the fact that in America we can stop acting like it's AD 55 because in effect most every American already *knows* about Christ—in other words, even if we do accept that converting every last Normie remains one of the most important things we have to do—what we're *still* left with is the fact that we're generally failing at it. If we accept that Christ, Paul, and others in the Bible are exhorting us to evangelize, we must then accept the idea that they're not telling us to be *unsuccessful* at it—that they're not saying, "Go forth, and spread the good news of the gospel—and make sure that you really alienate and offend people. Then report back here. We know it sounds weird—but trust us, there's a plan. Now get out there, and make people want to avoid Christians!"

Besides that we aren't living in AD 55, what's critical for us to remember about the act or process of evangelizing is that it's an endeavor that first and foremost must be *results oriented*. The charge to evangelize is not an absolute, interior command; it's not a private, personal imperative, such as "Be honest," "Don't steal," "Stop ogling your neighbor's wife," and so on. By definition those sorts of directives aren't subject to any kind of objective evaluative criteria: they're about things that *only* happen internally. Implicit in the directive to *evangelize*, however, is to produce quantifiable results; the idea is that the evangelizer actually *does* win people to Jesus. The fact that that's simply not or all too rarely happening means that at the very least it's time to seriously reconsider the message that we've for so long now been pressing upon our Normie brothers and sisters.

I believe we need to start sending the Normies a different message altogether. We need to do that because the message we're currently delivering unto them is doing exactly two things: keeping them away from us, and (since in actual, practical life we can't love someone we never even talk to) making it so that we can't possibly fulfill the Great Commandment.

Ouch

"I have no problem whatsoever with God or Jesus — only Christians. It's been my experience that most Christians are belligerent, disdainful, and pushy."—D. B., ATLANTA

"The main thing that baffles and angers me about Christians is how they can understand so little about human nature that when, in their fervor to convert another person, they tell that person (as they inevitably do, in one way or another), 'You're bad, and wrong, and evil,' they actually expect that person to *agree* with them. It pretty much guarantees that virtually the only people Christians can ever realistically hope to convert are those with tragically low self-esteem."—E. S., DENVER

"I have been a practitioner (and, in fact, what we call a 'priestess') of Paganism for twenty years. I came to the Pagan spiritual tradition because I found that mainstream Christian religion did not offer the support I needed to get through issues critical to women, such as domestic abuse, self-esteem, and women's political and economic rights in general. I was raised in the Methodist church, and taught that all I should expect for my life was to grow up, get married, have kids, obey my husband no matter what, and die. I could never accept this. I became involved in a violent alcoholic marriage, and the only woman-affirming path I could find was Paganism. The earth-based neopagan religions productively (and proactively) address women's issues and more, and gave me the positive reinforcement I needed to grow, change, and become what I never would have been otherwise: Free. I see current fundamentalist Christian religion as narrow minded, selfish, and currently practicing many of the things its own doctrine says it shouldn't. In other words, majorly hypocritical." —E.C., OMAHA, NE

"Whenever I'm approached by an evangelist—by a Christian missionary—I know I'm up against someone so obsessed and narrowly focused that it will do me absolutely no good to try and explain or share my own value system. I never want to be rude to them, of course, but never have any idea how to respond to their attempts to convert me; in short order, I inevitably find myself simply feeling embarrassed—first for them, and then for us both. I'm always grateful when such encounters conclude."
—K.C., FRESNO, CA

"I wish Christians would resist their aggressive impulses to morph others into Christians. Didn't Jesus preach that we should all love one another?"—M.G., SHORELINE, WA

Talk Amongst Yourselves

How comfortable are you trying to convert others to Christianity?

What's the biggest, most *instrumental* role that you personally have ever played in the conversion of another? How did the phenomenon of that transformation make you feel?

Do you think the reason most Normies aren't Christian has more to do with what they *do* know about our faith and the way it's practiced, or with what they don't?

If you were only allowed to ever say one single thing to any and all Normies about Christianity, what would it be? And what do you think the resistance to that singular thought would most often be?

Do you know any people who are practitioners of Wicca? Wanna bet?

3

What's Love Got to Do with It?

INSTEAD OF. "YOU NEED to become a Christian," I think a serious case can be made for the idea that the message we *should* be sending our nonbelieving friends and associates is, "We have free donuts!" When I first started going to church, I couldn't *believe* how often I found myself within biting distance of a decidedly ducky display of delectable donuts. And when I later worked for the Rescue Mission, I wasn't only amazed at the number of missionaries each church sponsored; I was also amazed at the number of *donuts* each church made available. Donuts on the coffee tables! Donuts on the side tables! Donuts on the conference tables! Donuts practically jammed into the pews with the Bibles and hymnals!

After about a month of working for the Rescue Mission, I had to change the message of my presentation from, "Please give me money to help feed the poor," to, "Please give me money so I can hire a personal trainer and try to lose some of this weight."

Stupid missions committees. You'd think, what with all the biblical emphasis on the righteousness of giving and all . . . but you'd be wrong. And it wasn't like the immediacy of my need wasn't readily apparent. But did pulling up my shirt and actually *showing* them my paunch help at all?

No.

You know, people *act* like they really want to help others, but when it comes down to actually hiring them a personal trainer, all of a sudden they . . .

Okay—that's enough of that routine.

Donuts in the pews was enough of that routine.

But the point is . . . well . . . actually, that we should simply offer people donuts really *is* kind of the point.

Because offering free donuts would be a gesture of pure, uncomplicated, we-expect-nothing-in-return affection.

Which in spirit would put us in line with the Great Commandment—Christ's one, overriding, clearly supreme directive for each and every one of us.

And here, just for review's sake, is that directive (from Mark 12:28-31):

> One of the teachers of the law came and heard [Jesus and some Sadducees] debating. Noticing that Jesus had given them a good answer, he asked him, "Of all the commandments, which is **the most important?"**
>
> **"The most important one,"** answered Jesus, "is this: 'Hear, O Israel, the Lord our God, the Lord is one. Love the Lord your God with all your heart and with all your soul and with all your mind and with all your strength.' The second is this: 'Love your neighbor as yourself.' **There is no commandment greater than these."**

(Humongous bold letters mine.)

All right, then. There it is. That's the Great Commandment.

So, let's think about the GC for a moment or eight. Clearly, this isn't something we want to just skim over.

It's not like we Christians can exactly ignore something that Jesus declared the most important commandment *ever*, right? Talk about your ultimate seal of approval. Just the *word* "commandment" makes me feel all . . . challenged and guilty.

But this isn't about me.

This is about Jesus, and his Absolute Order to us to love him with everything we've got, and to love our neighbors as we love ourselves. (Hmmm. Check it out: While I was typing those last few words, my next-door neighbor—a wiry guy with salt-and-pepper hair who always wears the same raggedy black sweater—started loudly screaming at his car. It's a thing he does fairly often: He paces around his poor old hooligan of an auto, and really *hollers* at it. So, as it happens, at this particular moment Mr. Scoldsmobile has given me even *more* reason to care about the Actual Practicality of part "B" of the Great Commandment.)

Well, Jesus' Great Commandment to love him mightily and our neighbor as ourselves doesn't seem very hard to grasp, does it? A child could understand that. It seems like about as simple a directive as we *can* get, outside of something like, "Have body hair," or "Think puppies are cute."

Actually, though, I don't think the Great Commandment is anywhere near as simple as it seems. I think, in fact, that (one of) the Secret Tricky Things about the GC is that it seems entirely *too* simple. I think one of the reasons the Great Commission gets so much more of our active attention than does the Great Commandment is because the Great Commandment seems so distinctly unchallenging.

It's like, "Love God with all my might? Done—I'm a Christian. Love my neighbor as I love myself? Done—I waved to my neighbor just yesterday when he was washing his car. Well, that was easy. *Now* what?"

Besides that it's Too Simple For Thought, another kind of

knee-jerk response most of us tend to have regarding the Great Commandment is automatically assuming that the two pronouncements comprising it aren't necessarily, or functionally, connected. "Love me" and "Love your neighbor" certainly sound as if they're two different things—like, "Brush your teeth every night," and "Floss your teeth every night." They seem kind of the same—but mostly different.

"Love God with all your might" seems like one thing; "Love your neighbor like he's you" seems like another.

And if most anyone else was saying those things, it's more than likely they really *would* be two different things, too.

But this is hardly anyone talking to us, eh?

This is the Ultimate Somebody, instead.

And if there's one thing you can say about Jesus, it's that he's not much of a word waster. He tends to be (He bless him) Exceptionally Succinct. If Jesus puts those two apparently separate directives that near one another, it's a safe bet he's hoping we'll derive something from the fact of their proximity.

It's a safe bet that he's *teaching* us something there.

You know how Jesus is. He teaches us something just by clearing his throat, or tying his sandal laces. About this, you just *know* he's being Joe Please Get This.

And I think what he desires for us to get is that not only are the two parts of the Great Commandment connected, they're *so* connected they can't even almost be separated. I think the idea behind Jesus' two-in-one mandate is that it's simply not possible to properly and effectively love our neighbor *until* we've given our full love to God.

I think that the most critical part of the Great Commandment is the part that Jesus, in his infinite wisdom, chose not to explicitly mention at all. That's just what great teachers do, isn't it? They give you, say, the letters L, V, and E—and leave it up to *you* to discover and place the O.

The part about the Great Commandment that Jesus doesn't articulate is what happens to us *between* the time we love him and the time we love our neighbor. What he doesn't say is how loving him with all of our heart, soul, and mind radically and completely (not to mention—oh, miracle!—quickly) transforms us. What he doesn't say is that before we are capable of giving absolute love to our neighbor we must first, and with all of our might, love him. What he doesn't say is that between giving the two kinds of Crucial Loves he does mention, we *receive* the most crucial love of all.

What Christ doesn't say—what he in fact leaves for us to discover on our own—is the degree to which the second part of the Great Commandment is dependent upon the first.

We're supposed to love God—which opens up our hearts so that we can feel how much God loves us—and *then* we're supposed to love our neighbor. That's it. That's the system we're in. That's how true and selfless love works. That's the *only* way we can truly love a person we don't really know all that well, if at all: We give our love to God; we get love from God (who, being the God he is, invariably gives us back about a zillion times more love than we gave); and then we pass that pure love along to whomever is lucky enough to next come our way.

And there we have it. *That's* how love makes (or is supposed to make) the world go round.

Let's try it. C'mon: Let's have ourselves a mini-Love Fest, right now. Take a moment, and with all the power in your heart and mind, love God. I'll do it, too.

Okay, I'm back.

Phenomenal.

So phenomenal, in fact, that you know what I feel like doing right now? I feel like going outside and *helping* my crazy neighbor yell at his car.

There *is* something about that car's Eastern Bloc Beige paint job that's never quite set right with me, actually. Might be nice to get that off my chest. Its hubcaps kind of annoy me, too, with their obnoxiously vulgar swells and dents.

Really, they're just wrong.

The point is: If just then you really did take a moment to love God with all of your might, then right now you're absolutely filled with absolute love. Because that's what *necessarily* happens when we love God. That's the extremely simple system we're all involved in: We get (way more) love from God than we give to God. What that means relative to the dynamic of the Great Commandment is the part of the GC that Jesus saw fit not to articulate—that he thought would be best for us to directly experience ourselves.

And when we have loved God with all of our heart, soul, and mind (and I think it's worth noting that this is the order in which Jesus put those three), and been rewarded a zillionfold by having our heart, soul, and mind filled with the reality of God's ineffable love, *how do we then find ourselves feeling about the world and everyone in it?*

Accepting!

We accept! We're . . . *okay* with everything, and everyone, exactly as they are.

We understand that first, foremost, and always, this is God's world.

We feel, to our bones, the majestic peace of divine acceptance.

From up on the mountaintop, all people look the same, don't they?

Ouch

"There are about a million things I'd like to say to Christians, but here's the first few that come to mind: Please respect my right to be the person I've chosen to become. Worship, pray, and praise your God all you want — but please leave me, and my laws, and my city, and my school alone. Stop trying to make me, or my children, worship your god. Why do we all have to be Christians? Respect my beliefs; I guarantee they're every bit as strong as yours. Mostly, please respect my free will. Let me choose if I want to marry someone of my own sex. Let me choose if I want to have an abortion or not. Let me choose to go to hell if that's where you believe I'm going. I can honestly say that I'd rather go to hell than live the hypocritical life I see so many Christians living." — D. B., SEATTLE

"I don't know whether or not most of the Christians I come across think they're acting and being like Jesus was — but if they do, they need to go back to their Bibles, and take a closer look at Jesus." — L. B., PHOENIX

"When did it become that being a Christian meant being an intolerant, hateful bigot? I grew up learning the positive message of Christ: Do well and treat others with respect, and your reward will be in heaven. Somehow, for a seemingly large group of Christians, that notion has gone lost: It has turned into the thunders and lights of the wrath of God, and into condemning everyone who disagrees with them to burning in the flames of hell. Somehow, present-day Christians forgot about turning the other cheek, abandoned the notion of treating others like they would like to be treated themselves; they've become bent on preaching, judging, and selfishly attempting to save the souls of others by condemning them. What happened to love? To tolerance? To respect?" — S. P., NASHVILLE

"The biggest problem I have with Christians is that I feel like I'm not accepted enough by them just for being a good person. I'm no thief, nor am I a liar or a killer. I do not wish harm on anyone—and yet to the Christian I'm a bad person for not accepting certain facets of their spirituality. In my heart I respect anyone who holds strong spiritual beliefs, as long as they respect my beliefs and the beliefs of others. My favorite Christians are those who will let me walk my own path, but are willing to provide guidance if I so need it. But no pushing on this path, please."—R. G., BELLINGHAM, WA

Talk Amongst Yourselves

Do you think that "Love your neighbor," and "Accept your neighbor unconditionally, *exactly* as they are" mean the same thing? Why or why not?

How do you understand the relationship between the two parts of the Great Commandment? Do you think they're essentially separate, or meant to be understood and experienced together?

As described on pages 49–50, the effect of being filled with God's love is to become essentially contemplative. But after you've prayed or meditated for a good long time, are you left feeling like that—or do you perhaps find yourself feeling more active in some way? If so, what sort of thing do you feel like doing?

Have you ever had a neighbor who yells at his car? Did you move, or call the police, or try to talk to the person, or what?

4

What's Love Got to Do with Us?

QUICK: WHAT'S THE THING in life that you want more than anything else in the world?

Well, sure, *now* you say love — but that's because you just saw the chapter title. If this chapter'd been titled, "Money, Money, Money, Mooooooooney — *(Money!)*" you'd have said, "Money."

Oh, you would too have.

You *would* have!

Oh, you reader-types. You're such an . . . independent lot.

Anyway, yes: The answer is love. Of course it is. And do you know *why* you want nothing in this world as much as you do love? Because you're human — and every single last one of us is exactly like that. You, me, your mother, your father, my sister, all of our aunts, uncles, cousins, neighbors, butchers, lawyers, hair stylists . . . no human being who ever has or ever will walk this planet wants anything more fervently or consistently than they do love.

That's right. I said lawyers. *No one* escapes the terrible, wonderful need for love that fuels the heart and soul of each and every one of us.

Love is so . . . massive.

Love is *so* massive that it is, in fact, God.

God Is Love.

It's more than just a bumper sticker, man. It's a 2,000-year-old theology.

So let us Christians consider here for a moment or two what it really means to us and our lives to say and believe that God is love. Because if God is love, then of course Jesus is love; and if Jesus tells us that we need to love our neighbors as we love ourselves, then, since he's the source of love, he *must* mean that we're supposed to love our neighbors with the same kind of unutterably pure love with which he loves us.

We love others as we're loved by God. That seems simple enough, right?

Right—except for when it doesn't, which is most all of the time. Because no matter how troubling it might be to admit, in our heart of hearts most of us know that accepting, processing, and giving love can make for some of the most difficult business of our lives. How could it possibly be otherwise? We are born desperately craving everything about love: Our furious need to receive and share it is an unceasing psychological (not to mention physical) hunger that's hardwired directly into our . . . motherboards.

Verily, are we all just love machines.

And what we as mature Christians understand is that (besides the love of the ones we love), the love we all *really* want—the love that each of us is in fact designed to desire—is the love of God.

Of course, back when we were children incapable of any thought more mature than "Feed Me Now," our parents *were* our gods: then (if not throughout our lives) we certainly desired their love. And it was in turn their precious lot in life to make sure that we received their positive, nurturing love: Their job was to model healthy human-to-human love—and to also, slowly but surely, turn our hearts, minds, and eyes upward toward that divine love which, by their example and teaching, they would help us to understand informs and ultimately surpasses all others.

Man. Tough gig to get just right, no? No wonder so many of us grew up with parents who fell short of being the kind of parents we *wish* they'd been. Too bad so many of us had parents who, instead of modeling and teaching us good love, bequeathed unto us a version of human and godly "love" that lacked that certain, shall we say, sane something.

Many of our parents were not, alas, exactly church-going types.

Or maybe they were, but their understanding of their faith was wanting in some crucial ways.

Maybe they had no faith in anything, and lived their lives in fear.

Maybe as kids they never had any control over anything, and spent the rest of their lives furiously trying to make up for that.

Maybe they were so poor just feeding us anything edible was all they cared about.

Maybe what they really wanted was a good *dog*. Who knows what makes people end up the way they do? All we really can know is that during the early part of our lives — the part where we were learning all the really vital, core emotional stuff that was destined to stay with us like marrow in a bone — a lot of us weren't given the emotional and spiritual tools we should have been in order to have learned how best to receive and give both human and divine love. And for many of us, that critical deficiency resulted in the morphing of our natural yearning for Good Love into what amounts to an unnatural craving for all of this world's (Ultimately Disappointing) ever-seductive substitutes for good love: for food, money, power, fame, and so on.

As the saying I'm right now making up goes, a starving man will eat anything.

As Confucius would have said if he'd thought of it: Love averted is love perverted.

Like the poet once said: As want becomes need, so love becomes greed.

Okay, fine: We'll leave poetry to the (real) poets. But that last one did, at least, point to exactly why, for most of us, the whole subject of love is pretty profoundly . . . touchy.

Wanting something is one thing; *needing* that same thing is, of course, another altogether. And because so early on in our lives so many of us had installed into our core selves the "knowledge" that we'd never get enough of the kind of pure love we (at some level) knew we'd need in order to be truly happy, a lot (dare I say most?) of us at one time or another in our lives went into what amounts to Survival Mode, where (and usually with, God knows, more help than we should have had) we actually reconfigured our nature, in the hopes of becoming someone — or in the hopes of at least successfully *pretending* to become someone — who doesn't really want or need much if any love at all.

And thus did some of us become, say, the Strong and Silent type.

Or the Porno Girl.

Or the drug addict.

Or the workaholic.

Or the (dare I say it?) Holier-Than-Thou Christian.

Or we adopted some other persona no better at handling life than the True Self that willed it into existence — and which then began to hide behind it.

Sometimes, when we can't get something we need, we summon up the power to become someone who doesn't need that thing at all. That's how a lot of us *make* it through difficult times of our lives. That's how as kids many of us effectively rose above conditions that would otherwise have done us in.

And then later in our lives, of course, that's also how a lot of us crash back down again. Because rarely, if ever, is the person whom we made ourselves become in order to survive our childhood the same person who is prepared or equipped to successfully handle our adulthood.

Initially, for instance, we may learn to pretend that we're callous cynics — and then later find ourselves unable to respond emotionally in the manner our life mates need. And then what do we do? *Then* whom do we become?

If most of us, as children, didn't get enough of the kind of love we should have, then as adults most of us face the same problem: How do we begin believing in the kind of pure love that out of necessity (and habit) we've spent our lives believing doesn't exist at all?

Stupid parents. Why couldn't they have been the enlightened spiritual geniuses they were *supposed* to be? Why did they have to give us . . . *their* doinked-up version of love?

Man, is this ever something I know something about.

Talk about having Wrong Parents.

Yeah, that's right. I have issues, man.

What of it? I'm not afraid to admit it.

As it happens, I've got more issues than *TV Guide*, Bucko! So just *back off.*

Oh, wait: Sorry about that last part. That's just part of my whole defensive apparatus. I'm working on smoothing that away.

But seriously. *TV Guide.*

I know what you're thinking: "You, John? Issues? Surely, you jest! You're one of the most intellectually and spiritually gifted people I've ever not actually met. The fact that you would declare yourself to have 'issues' only makes you that much more lovable! God, how I long to possess you. Where do you live? What's your home address? Tell me. 'Cuz I'll find out anyway. Oh, trust me: I'll find out. Why don't you save us both some trouble, and just tell it to me now?"

Um. Yeah.

So, it's come to this: Now I'm actually stalking myself. In print.

I'm telling you: Issues!

What's that? Still doubt that I'm a charter member of the Psycho for Life Club? Really? How kind of you. Wrong, but kind. And to prove it, let's take a moment to examine the evidence, shall we? Let's look, in a nutshell, at my claim to a nut's hell.

My Very Real Case for Being a Very Real Case

My father ditched out on his/our happy, middle-class suburban life when I was eight years old. (And this was long enough ago so that once their marital vows became mutual "Ciao!"s, my mom and dad *easily* became the only divorced parents in the neighborhood. It was so weird being, suddenly, the kid with the radically unnatural home life.) *Poof!* Instant Dad-B-Gone! One minute I was part of a nuclear family—Father, Mother, eleven-year-old sister Nancy, seven-year-old little Bro (me), dog, cat, hamster, guinea pig—and the next my family just *went* nuclear.

My dad moved into a one-bedroom *bachelor pad* some twenty miles from the suburban tract home in which my mom, sister, and I continued to live.

At least we got to stay in our house. That was . . . nice.

Except that two years after my dad left that very house, my *mom* left it, too.

I was, like, "What the *hell?* Is it the green shag carpet? *Cuz we can* change *that, you know!*"

First, as part of our happy, whole family, our mother was (more or less) Donna Reed herself; next, liberated from what she took to calling her "emotionally retarded" ex-husband, she rather instantly transformed into a pot-smoking, rap-session-going, Vietnam-war-protesting *college student.* And then, two years into being a single mother (and a real babe of one, at that: believe me, you haven't lived until you've watched a succession of *college professors* nervously fidgeting on your couch as they wait for their date with your *mom* to kick in), she became no mother at all, because she totally disappeared.

"I'm going to the store for some milk and bread," she said to my sister and me one sunny afternoon around one o'clock. She took her keys, purse, and sunglasses from off the dining table. "Be right back!" she said, closing the door behind her.

And then it was three o'clock, and she hadn't come home yet. Pretty weird.

Then it was six o'clock, and she still hadn't come home. Pretty *darn* weird.

Then it was eight o'clock, and dark—and still no mom. Okay. Completely freakish.

Then it was midnight, and Nancy and I were just frantic with worry. (I have no idea why neither of us thought to call the police. Well, I know *I* didn't because I had no idea cops even *did* stuff like find lost moms. If my sister—who was thirteen by then—thought to alert the authorities, it makes sense, given the severely disturbing way my mother had begun treating her once our father had left, that she just might freakin' not.)

Next morning—still no mom!

But then guess who *did* show up back in our house the next

morning? Our dad! After two years away, our six-foot-four, two hundred and twenty pound *dad* just . . . turned the front door key, walked on in, and was home again.

About the first thing he saw upon his Big Entrance was my sister and I more or less huddled together on the couch, scarfing Oreos. After prying us off him he said, "Kids, I need to talk to you."

We were definitely all ears.

"Now Nancy, John," he said, "What I have to tell you isn't . . . very easy to say. Your mother has, it seems, um . . . taken a little vacation. She's not going to be living here anymore. I'm not sure exactly where she *is* going to be living — in fact, I'm not sure where she's gone to at all, or what's happened to her. I'm sure she's fine, though. The main thing for you to know is that I'm back now, and that I'm going to be taking care of you from now on, or until we can figure out what's going on with your mother. For now, everything's going to continue exactly as it was before — except for without your mother. Now come on — you kids need to get to school."

Yeah. What we really needed right then was a *geography lesson.*

What made the whole event particularly . . . different, is that when our dad came back to live with us, he brought with him someone *else* to live with us, too. It turned out he'd gotten (surprise!) *married,* to a fairly tall, square-shouldered, bombshell-figured, ramrod-backed, blue-eyed woman wearing, when we met her, form-fitting Capri jeans, a sunny sleeveless blouse, and a blonde wig coiffed into something that managed to say at once, "I'm a healthy, fun person you can depend on," and, "Are you sure you don't have any Jews hiding in your basement?"

Maybe five minutes after introducing his new wife to us

(which he did upon our return home from school on the day of his return), my dad and she asked if my sister and I would mind calling her "Mom."

I looked at my sister, clutching to her chest her binder adorned with Flower Power stickers. If she could call this new woman "Mom," then I could. But I saw that just then Nancy had lapsed into "Brain Overload: Can't Talk" mode. So I jumped in. "Sure," I said. "No problem. Mom." I tried to smile when I said it. I have no idea what expression actually appeared on my face.

The next morning—a Saturday, her first in her new/our old home—"Mom" backed me alone into a corner of my bedroom. With her face very close to mine, and in a voice kept low but infused with a kind of feral menace I'd *sure* never heard from an adult before, she said, "I want you to listen to me, John. You and your sister mean absolutely nothing to me. The only thing the three of us have in common is your father. I never wanted a family; I *never* wanted children. I'm here for two reasons only: because I love your father, and I love this house. This house is worth something—and in ten years, it'll be worth more. Just like your sister, you're welcome to stay in this house until you're eighteen, but not a day after that. And while you live here, you need to make sure this house—*my* house—doesn't deteriorate in value." She shot a look at the posters on my wall—a Sierra Club poster of some pretty woods that said, "In Wildness is the Preservation of the Earth," a copy of "Desiderata," a hippie-style black light poster of Buddha, and so on. "These come down today," she said. "I don't want you to put anything on these walls again. The tack holes detract from the value of the house." She glared hard at me; I remember thinking she was going to bite me—and God knows she had the choppers to get the job done. "Do we understand each other?"

I think I managed to nod. I'm not entirely sure I didn't pee my pants.

And then "Mom" was gone — off, I assumed, to clue my sister into The New Reality.

And it was just after she left me alone in my room again that I discovered what I would not, in a million years, have ever thought possible: I could actually miss my real mom even *more* than I had been.

What had happened to our real mom was something Nancy and I wouldn't find out for two years after she'd left — after, for us, Life 3.0 had begun. During those two years neither my sister nor I heard so much as a peep from our mother: We didn't know if she was dead, or had run away, or what. No phone call. No note. No visit in the middle of the night. No secret, coded, critical little communiqué that I was forever desperately searching to discern. Just . . . silence. Nothing.

As gone as gone gets.

To this day, whenever I see parents on TV who have a child who's been abducted or disappeared, I always think, "God, I can't imagine how that feels" — and then remember that, actually, I can.

And you don't *even* want to be my wife coming home from somewhere later than she said she'd be back. Poor thing. If she's, like, an hour late from somewhere, and didn't *call* so I wouldn't worry, I can totally milk my Serious Abandonment Issues to get free foot rubs out of her for a week.

It's wrong, I know.

Issues! TV Guide!

(Oh — as it turned out, our mother hadn't "disappeared" at all. She had, instead, been all along living and working [as a librarian!] only a few miles away from our house. For those whole two years, she'd essentially been right up the street! Upon reentering our lives ["Son," my dad said to me one day after I'd come home from a Little League baseball practice, "your mother called"—and just like that I was on my knees], my mom explained to me how she had needed to get away to "find" herself; it turned out that, as she put it, "God never wanted me to be a mother." And her idea whilst finding herself had been to remain utterly hidden from the children God never intended her to have, so as not to interfere with Nancy and me settling into the life that God apparently *did* intend for us as a correction to his earlier mistake. It was right around her Big Return that Nancy and I also learned that our father had, in fact, known all along where our mother was—he'd been in regular contact with her, we learned—but that he never told us what he knew, because he felt it would be less painful for us to imagine that our mother somehow *couldn't* communicate with us, than it would be to know that she could, but simply chose not to. He was dead wrong about that—any closure beats no closure—but you can't blame a guy for trying, eh?)

My sister Nancy ditched out of our home when she was but fifteen (and without question that was the Suddenly Missing Immediate Family Member that wounded me the most). I managed to gut it out until I was sixteen.

And then—early out of high school, living in a big city sixty miles away, trying to sell encyclopedias door-to-door in what amounted to a huge, blighted ghetto—my Fun Life Ride *really* began.

So, issues? Yeah, I got issues, baby. I've got more issues than *TV Guide*. That's right. I used the same joke three times. *And I don't care.* That's how [very bad word]-ed up *I* am.

I don't want to go into this *too* much more, since this book isn't *Memoirs of a Geeksha* or anything, but my less-than-ideal childhood really did tweak me up pretty good. It definitely installed in me some basic assumptions about people and life that didn't exactly make for a first-class, one-way ticket to Happyville. For instance: To me, in my mind, an absolute Core Truth that I learned about life is ALL THE REALLY IMPORTANT THINGS RADICALLY CHANGE IN WAYS YOU CAN'T POSSIBLY ANTICIPATE OR PREDICT.

Which is to say: NOBODY STAYS.

Which is to say: LOVE IS ALWAYS SUSPECT, AND ABSOLUTELY CONDITIONAL.

Which (free foot rubs or not) is not a good assumption to have hardwired into your consciousness, sub- or otherwise. It pretty much guaranteed that whenever I took one of those "What kind of job should you have when you grow up?" aptitude tests, the results would show that, rather than an accountant, lawyer, or fireman, I was born to be a slovenly, drug-addled shut-in. "Love is Disappointing Crap" just isn't the kind of Life Schema that equips one to . . . well . . . get a life. (For starters, it completely disconnects one's Plan For The Future wiring. It sure did in my case, anyway. I couldn't plan for my future if I was standing on railroad tracks and off in the distance heard a distinct "Choo-choo!" In my head, it's so absolutely undependable that it's actually impossible for me to think about the future at all. Whenever I try to, it just . . . dissolves. It's like the Planning Gene fell off my DNA helix, or something. I don't know what I'm going to do tomorrow, and the idea of seriously planning what I might be doing five or ten years from now is so far beyond my way of processing information that it's like asking me to start dreaming at night in Chinese. I simply can't. I just don't know that language.)

So that's (part of) my personal trip.

My (phenomenal) wife was raised in circumstances so

gut-wrenchingly miserable it's Beyond Unfathomable that she's not a frothing ax-murderer. Just thinking about her childhood makes me want to run my head into a wall.

One of my best friends watched his father commit suicide by shooting off his head with a shotgun. (At home. In his living room. While he, my friend, and his other son — my friend's older brother — were watching a football game together. At the moment it happened, my friend's brother was in the kitchen, getting some chips. My friend was so close he got splattered.)

Another one of my friends spent his tenth year with his mom lying on the couch in their living room, while she slowly but surely died of stomach cancer.

I have a friend who, as a kid, was in his bedroom when, out in the family room, his father (loudly) murdered his mistress.

I have a great friend who, as an *infant*, was regularly beaten by his father so badly that finally Child Protection Services came and took him away.

I'm very close to a woman whose mother, when the two of them were alone in the house together, used to force her, for hours at a time, to eat chocolate until she threw up.

You get the idea: Life, in a lot of ways, for a lot of people, is . . . emotionally challenging, to say the least.

And, as I say, I don't think life's like that for *some* people, but rather for most. It sure is for all of them I've ever taken the time to get to know really well, anyway. And I don't think it's just because I'm the object of some bizarre-o "Let's Make John Only Meet Dysfunctional People" plan that God's executing because he got bored trying to come up with a new design for lizards, or whatever. I think it's because most all of us had parents who . . . well, let's say, had their own issues. And for sure that's (what let's here call) natural; for *sure* that's life. But what it means is that most of us were left not being anywhere near as good as we might be at getting and giving the kind of clear, uncomplicated, unadulterated love that all people need.

And in real, practical terms, what *that* always boils down to is that most of us don't feel very lovable at all.

Because when we were young we didn't get the kind of love we should have, most of us, at the core of our beings, feel, to one degree or another, that we don't deserve love at all.

And there you have it: Life in a nutshell for . . . what . . . 96 percent of us? 95? 94?

Okay, ninety-four is as low as I'm going. Because that would mean *6 percent* of us are enjoying Optimum Psychological and Spiritual Health.

And then for sure I would have met at least *one* such person in my life.

Then again, maybe I have. How would I know? When you're wearing green spectacles, everyone looks green.

But I don't think that's it. I think just about all of us *are* green. I think *everyone* has a Serious Issue or thirty-two that they're relatively better or worse at hiding from the world. It's been my experience that just about every single one of us, at the deepest levels of our beings, thinks or fears that when it comes right down to it, we're a broken, neglected toy left a very long time ago on the Island of Misfits.

It's a hard thing to say. And God knows it's a hard way for any of us to live.

And it's certainly something about which endless books have been written — the Self Help section at my local Borders practically stretches to the border of the next state. And I sure ain't meanin' to turn this book into another one of them kinda books. Except in this sense, I have to: If God's commanded us to love our neighbors as we love ourselves, then without a doubt it's incumbent upon us to discover just how much, and in just what way, we do, in fact, love ourselves. Because it's easy to assume that when the Great Commandment says, "Love your neighbor as you love yourself," what it *means* is, "Love your neighbor absolutely—in the same way that you love yourself absolutely." Which would be great, and easy—except for the little, tiny, massive fact that most of us *don't* love ourselves absolutely. For most of us, that's just not how it works. That's not where we're at.

That's just not who we are.

When I go out into the world, I don't usually do so consciously aware of myself as a vessel of God's love. I usually go out into the world consciously aware of myself as someone who should at least shave their *neck* every once in a while. I go out consciously aware that my hips are stinging like they're on fire, because, unbelievably enough, I'm actually outgrowing my *fat* pants.

Issues, baby! Like TV Guide!

I don't go out like a divine being awash in God's love. I go out like an earthbound mortal struggling to feel lovable.

And yet I also go as one commanded by Jesus Christ to love my neighbor as I love myself.

Hmmm.

Interesting dynamic, no?

I don't think I've ever heard the words, "Love your neighbor as you love yourself" without thinking, "Well, yeah. But, depending on how much you love yourself." Given how difficult it is for any of us to ever show someone else more love than we happen to be feeling for ourselves, I can't see my way around the idea that in fairly short order the Great Commandment becomes as much about self-esteem as it is about anything else.

Ouch

"I grew up Jewish in a Southern Baptist town, where I was constantly being told that I killed Christ, ate Christian babies, and was going to hell. So I learned early that many Christians have — or sure seem to have — no love in their hearts at all. It also seems so odd to me that Christians think that if I don't accept their message my ears and heart are closed, because it seems to me like *they* have excessively closed ears and hearts to anyone else's spiritual message and experience. They seem to have no sense of the many ways in which God reaches out to everyone. As far as I've ever known, Christians are narrow in their sense of God, fairly fascistic in their thinking, and extremely egotistical in thinking God only approves of them." — B. P., HOUSTON

"I think that the discomfort that I always feel whenever a Christian offers me 'salvation' has to do with a distortion of the normal act of gift giving. When I give a gift, my sole hope is that the recipient enjoys it. My ego's not involved at all; my giving is a selfless act. But when a Christian is trying to 'give' the word of their Lord, there's something in it for them, too. They're not thinking only of the other person: They also want something from the transaction. In that sense they're like telemarketers: They offer you something that they say will benefit you, but in fact *they* benefit if you take what they're giving. That's not really giving at all — and I think explains why it so rarely works. At the very least, giving in the spirit of getting is impolite." — G. M., CHICAGO

"I know that at heart I'm a Christian, but I just can't stand to have someone come up to me and slam Christ in my face. Showing someone the benefits of Christianity is fine, but shoving

it in their face as if they need Jesus as much as they need oxygen in their next breath is enough to make even me—someone with no doubt that God is there and calling him—backtrack and look for a place to hide. The absolute worst are the people who refer to God in every other sentence, and then act like the biggest heathens in the world—as if claiming God gives them a license to do as they please (i.e., a 'born again' former co-worker of mine who was forever borrowing money he never repaid). It's no wonder people run when they see Christians coming: Half of them are absolute in-your-face radicals, and the other half are manipulating liars who seem to have no clue who God is."
—E. W., ST. LOUIS

"I had a friend who was, as they say, reborn. During my breaks from college she invited me to her church, and I did go a couple of times. In a matter of a month, at least ten people at her church told me that I was going to hell. The ironic thing is that I do believe in God; I've just never found a church where I felt at ease. However, in their eyes, I was nothing but a sinner who needed to be saved. I stopped going to that church (which in the past four years has grown from a small to a megachurch), but in time, through my friend, have seen some of these people again. None of them ever fails to treat me exactly as they did four years ago. All I can say is this: Constantly telling someone they're going to hell is not a good way to convert them."—A. S., CHICAGO

"Religion always seemed too personal for me to take advice about it from people I don't know."—D. P., DENVER

Talk Amongst Yourselves

Do you think you have in your own life any Fundamental Operating Principles that you've always just assumed are a universal truth for everyone's life, but that are actually the result of something *wrong* about life that you learned a long, long time ago?

Do you think that as a child anyone avoids the kind of emotional trauma that to some extent they spend the rest of their lives trying to recover from?

What do you think the relationship is between those issues within us that to whatever degree keep us from feeling lovable, and God's love for us?

Do you think that no matter how filled with God's love you might be, there are still some things that you just couldn't forgive a person for doing?

Do you think that when Jesus told us to love our neighbor as we love ourselves, he was, in fact, asking us to consider how much we do or don't love ourselves?

Doesn't just hearing about the author's difficult childhood make you want to hug him? And isn't sending cash, check, or a money order really just another way of saying you care?

5

So Being Born Again
Isn't the Same as Being Mature?

IT SEEMS TO ME that there are only two ways for us to in any consistent way live our lives in the spiritual/psychological place we need to if we're going to love our neighbors in the absolute, unconditional way that God loves us. The first is by taking the Directly Spiritual path: by opening our hearts to God's love for us, and then shining that same love on our neighbors. Whenever we're talking to virtually anyone — our spouse, our kids, our next-door neighbor, a coworker, a total stranger — we need to right then and there open our hearts to the glorious, ennobling joy of the Holy Spirit within us.

Because of course that is how we finally *do* get enough love: We go right to the source.

And if while talking to someone we access the Holy Spirit and get filled with God's love, then how lucky for that person! See how our breathing slows down as the peace of the Lord settles upon us! See how we suddenly find ourselves caring more about the emotional well-being of the person with whom we're talking than we do about whatever it is we're talking with them about! See how our whole conversation with them shifts into one that's much richer, and more personal!

Ahhhh. One moment of Holy Spirit Infusion, and like *that* we become . . . well, kind of pretty darn Christlike.

So. Accessing the Holy Spirit is one way to go. And—as we all know—doing that is one Instantaneous Bahamarama.

But as I've said, connecting to the Holy Spirit within us sure can't be the *only* way we give real love to others, because, in practical terms, that's just not enough. I mean, in any given moment it *is* enough, of course; in any given moment, the Holy Spirit is a great deal more than enough. But there's simply no way that you, or I, or anyone else in this world is going to stop and fill ourselves with the Holy Spirit every time we interact with another person. That's just the fact of it. That's just not the way we . . . interact with reality.

We can spend an hour every morning praying, reading the Bible, and being with the Holy Spirit, and every time we talk to somebody we can do our best to open ourselves up to the power of the Holy Spirit (and, God knows, all those things are wonderful), but the bottom line is that during the course of a great majority of the time we spend with others, all that we're going to be is just . . . us.

Us.

Ourselves.

Who we are.

As we are.

As we willed ourselves to become. (And, let us never forget, as we *had* to will ourselves to become. Yay for Survival 101!)

It's mostly just us out there. Unplugged.

And out there we're going to meet and interact with people in our Full Persona Mode, because that's how life *works*. Every time I talk to a "neighbor" out in the Big Bad World somewhere, I'm not going to have the time—or the presence of mind to take the time—to fill myself up with the Holy Spirit just before or as I'm talking to that person. That's just not going to happen. Most of the time it's just gonna be me, my (psycho-making) background, and whatever personality resources I can muster in order to come across as a normal, good-natured, well-adjusted person who *isn't* about to run screaming into the street for no apparent reason. (Or, in my case, who couldn't even plan to do that.)

So. What do I do about *those* sorts of times? What do I do about all those times when I want to love my neighbor with the proper spirit, but the Big Spirit doesn't happen to be big within me just then? How do I fly right, when instead of letting God be my co-pilot, I've effectively—in one of the many, many ways I'm so "naturally" inclined to—disconnected his microphone, and so now am not listening to him at all?

Again: Therein lies the rub.

Well, there*out* lies the rub, really. Because—if I could just say this, even though I know it runs contrary to the thinking of some of our prominent Christian Leaders—it's my little tiny, little eensie-weensy opinion that Christianity today has it dead wrong when it insists that there is no proper place in the life of Christians for the appreciation of what so many of us have learned to disdainfully dismiss as "secular" psychology or psychotherapy.

Gotta little story 'bout psychotherapy. Like ta' hear it? Here it go:

Once, about two years after I became a Christian—so when I was somewhere around forty years old—I found myself thinking that it might be a good idea for me to go see a shrink. Some of that truly difficult stuff from my childhood was still with me (like it's possible for it *not* to be), and even though it was clear enough that some of the Less Than Helpful ways I was thinking and acting as a forty-year-old man were connected to that stuff, I found myself incapable of taking care of it myself: That particular set of roots was just too deep for me to dig out on my own.

So I started to see a therapist. The guy I went to was totally nice: kind, thoughtful, funny, patient with his patients. I enjoyed our sessions: Where else but in therapy do you get to talk endlessly about *nothing* but yourself, without ever once having to worry about being insufferably boring and rude, since the other person's whole *job* is to do nothing but listen to you? It's pretty much a dream come true—especially for me, since so much of my dream life happens to involve me getting interviewed on some hugely popular talk show.

Issues! TV—oh, forget it.

One day, after I'd gone to see Dr. Izzy Listening maybe four times, I was having lunch with the pastor of my church—and, in small-talk mode, he asked me how I was doing—and I said fine, and how one interesting thing that was happening was that I had started to see a psychotherapist.

Pastor Mike stopped his tuna sandwich in the air halfway toward his mouth. "You've what?" he said.

"Started to see a psychotherapist." He looked at me like I'd said something about starting to see Psycho the Rapist. "You know," I said, "a shrink. Asks about your mom. Shows you inkblots. Surreptitiously checks out your fingernails to see if you've been gnawing them like a manic chipmunk. Like Frasier, on TV. Except not as funny."

Mike slowly lowered his sandwich to his plate. "You're seeing a therapist?" he asked. "A *psycho*therapist?" He said it like he was saying, "Your brother died? Bob?" or "You have cancer? Of the brain?"

"Well, yeah," I said. "Why? Is that bad? Is there some sort of national ban on shrinks going on that I missed hearing about?"

Mike's expression as he quietly regarded me triggered a technicolor flashback: Suddenly I was back in elementary school, sitting in the office of Mr. Huber, our school's principal. And I don't mean sitting in the outer, main part of Mr. Huber's office, either, where his secretary Bunny worked. (Right—like I'd make that name up.) Oh, sure, like any normal kid with a pretty good throwing arm and a still-evolving sense of when a teacher is or isn't watching him, I'd done my time parked on the little Bad Student Bench situated right across from Bunny's desk. (I liked ol' Bunny. She used to share her Hostess cupcakes with me. I used to not be able to help thinking what a great mom for me she would make.) But this time I was past that Amateur Riff-Raff grounding station; this time my transgressions had landed me at Ground Zero for Troubleville. This time—and for, like, the third time—my apprehended hiney was in the inner sanctum of Mr. Huber's actual, private office—with the aquarium, floor-to-ceiling wooden bookcases, and the carpet so thick that upon entering the room this latest time I had momentarily considered trying to hide in it.

And there, looming down upon me from over the vast expanse of his desk, was Principal Huber's giant face. And *that* was where I'd seen the expression that I was now getting from my beloved church pastor, Mike.

It was an expression that communicated . . . well, this: "I'm worried about you, son. I like you a great deal, and am deeply pained by how little that's going to help you, should you persist in continuing down the same terrible road upon which you are currently traveling. How in God's name did a person as seemingly intelligent as yourself ever come to be so tragically misdirected? I fear for you; I fear for the heart of anyone who ever has, or ever will, care about you."

"What is it?" I said to Mike. "What's up?"

"Well, John," he said softly, lowering his sandwich back to his plate. "Don't you think the Bible is all the therapy you need? Don't you think Jesus is the best psychotherapist there is?"

And so began the conversation wherein I first learned what I've

since learned is very true indeed: (Some) Christians don't like psychology, or psychotherapy, or Freud, or the phrase, "So, why don't
you tell me about your mother?" or anything at all having to do
with the idea of Regular People ("trained" or not) mucking around
with the kinds of all-critical Core Human Issues that they believe
should be brought before God for their resolution, and God alone.
Such Christians think that psychology is a tool used by secular
humanists to convince people that in order to be happy they don't
need the saving grace of Christ any more than they do a lucky
rabbit's foot or little sack of mugwort worn around their necks,
that the applied methodologies of the psychological disciplines are
perfectly capable of bringing them the same level of peace and
fulfillment that Christians get from knowing Christ.

"Who needs religion?" say the psychologists. "We've got
the mind!"

"Who needs psychologists?" say the Christians. "We've
got *God!*"

"Who knew either side had any opinion at all about the other?"
says I. "I've got a *headache.*"

Listen: I'm not meaning to in any way denigrate or make
fun of the idea that Christ *is* the ultimate shrink. (Oh — and do
let me say right here that of course I understand that a great
many Christians hold views radically different from those of
Pastor Mike. I know not all Christians scorn psychology; I know
that there are, in fact, a ton of Christian psychologists out there
with thriving practices. It's a big world, no doubt about it. Many
Christians. Many ideas. One love [I hope].) Of course Christ
is the King of Healers. But as far as I can see, one of the things
about having a relationship with Jesus is that it really *is* a relationship, and just like I can't expect my wife to pull all the weight

in the relationship between her and me, I can't expect Jesus to pull all the weight in the relationship between him and me.

If I want my relationship with Jesus to be all that it can be, then I have to help; I have to *do* stuff to make that happen. And one of the things I have to do—and I'm arguing it's *the* thing, given the awesome weight Jesus placed on the Great Commandment—is to rid myself of anything and everything standing between me and the love God wants me to accept from him and then pass along to others.

And by "me" here, I don't mean the Holy Spirit within me. Of course the Holy Spirit within me can connect with the unadulterated love of God; it *is* the unadulterated love of God. I mean the . . . other me—the one I built up *around* the Holy Spirit.

The one whose eyes tend to focus more on earth than heaven.

The one I created for, in fact, that very purpose.

The one I became; the one whom I fashioned to essentially block what amounts to the unadulterated love of God.

I've got to get *all* of me that's in the way of Jesus out of the way. I've got to clear the road to my purest heart, so that Jesus' love can take its natural place there, and from there radiate outward, and do its miraculous thing. Properly obeying Jesus' greatest commandment to us means purposefully and consciously eradicating everything within us that at any given moment of our lives keeps us from experiencing the fullness of God's love—which we must experience, in order to then fully love our neighbors.

We need to get busy dismantling the (natural! helpful!) persona we developed in order to survive whatever weirdo upbringing we had to endure.

As Christians, consciously connecting to God's love via the Holy Spirit is half of the obligation (and pleasure) we must accept in order to fulfill the Great Commandment—and it's certainly the easier half. Learning to get rid of everything that's *interfering* with that love is the other half. And that part of Doing Our Share isn't so easy. Because we can pour over the concordance or index in the back of our study Bibles until our eyes bleed, and we're never going to see any entries such as, "Mother—insanely invasive and clinically narcissistic," or "Father—profoundly immature; lashes out physically."

There's no "Older Sister—nearly frenetic, but unrequited love for."

Jesus never said anything about any of our particular problems. But it's our special, extremely unique problems — *our* parents, *our* upbringing, the underlying source of *our* insecurities—that *we* have to deal with on a conscious, practical, rational, issue-by-issue basis, if we're going to get all the *muck* of it out of the way of God's love.

All that nasty, counterproductive stuff from our past is real, and it happened, and for as long as we pretend like it didn't happen or doesn't bother us, it will necessarily continue to clog the pipeline between our hearts and the Holy Spirit's love. God wants us to heal from that stuff—but we've got to cooperate with that process. For a lot of us, there are things in our hearts and minds that are so intensely personal, and so deeply rooted within us, that even Jesus can't touch them unless *we* grab hold of them first.

One of the hardest truths of our lives is that whatever we built—or, more precisely, whatever was built in our hearts and minds *for* us — *we* must disassemble, and neutralize.

We don't have to do it with a shrink. (I didn't; it's through the amazing love and character of my wife that I've made whatever progress I have toward what amounts to consciously and willingly accepting God's love for me.) But we *do* have to do it. I think too many Christians rely upon the Holy Spirit to do all their emotional heavy lifting for them. But that's not the Holy Spirit's function — and to insist that it is or should be is like trying to use an aardvark for a pack mule: it's bound to make for a long, difficult trip. In order for us to be right with God — much less for us to arrange someone *else* being right with God — we've got to haul out our *own* emotional baggage. *We've* got to open ourselves wide to the Power that can enable us to clean up that mess within us that belongs, exclusively, to us.

And for an awful lot of us, that right there is a veritable lifetime of work. And, to be perfectly clear: There *is*, of course, no better coworker than God/Jesus/the Holy Spirit. Once we start rearranging our interior selves, we have only to ask, and our Best Friend Ever Jesus will pitch right in and make sure that that job gets done right. It's just that *we* have to initiate that work; for what will probably be the only time in our lives, *we're* then in the position of having to direct the Holy Spirit to do the work that needs doing. (Yikes! Us, as God's . . . job supervisor! My advice is: Whenever Jesus wants to go to lunch or take off early, let him.)

I think that rather than spend any more time worrying about the specks in anyone else's eyes, we should all just close our own eyes (planks and all), and ask God's help in cleaning up everything within us that's standing between our truer selves and the Holy Spirit. Let's just worry about doing that for a while. Let's just trust that if we do that — and if when we do we follow up on whatever Inside Information comes of it — then, like day follows night, God will take care of every thing, and every person, in this whole, great big wide world of his.

Ouch

"I was raised in the Midwest as a Roman Catholic; I spent eight years in a R.C. grade school and four in a small, excellent R.C. girls' high school. As a result of my education, I know a fair amount about Christianity. I now live in South Carolina and am basically appalled at how often I'm lectured to by Christians here who have no knowledge whatsoever of the cultural, literary, political, or historical frames of reference in which the Bible is best read and understood. What's even worse is the degree to which they are uninterested in learning anything more than the painfully little they do about the faith to which they pledge such fervent allegiance. The other day I actually had a Christian ask me whether or not Jews believed in God. Unbelievable—yet typical." —N. D., [TOWN WITHHELD UPON REQUEST], SOUTH CAROLINA

"I think of myself as an open-minded spiritual seeker. I have no beef with Jesus or what he taught, nor with churches generally. What I take exception to are the spiritual blinders so many Christians seem so intent on wearing. I feel like it's exactly because I'm open-minded—because I'm willing to see the validity in different approaches to the divine—that so many Christians seem unable to respect me as much as I know I at least try to respect them." —C. H., SEATTLE

"For me, religion is an extremely personal thing, as I believe it should be for everyone. I am sincerely happy for people who have a strong connection with God, or who have experienced life-changing, sudden revelations that gave them unbreakable faith. When someone tells me such a story about themselves I'm intrigued, moved, and honestly glad to hear it. But it's still their story. Their moment. Their faith. While that experience swept in and turned their world upside down, it really doesn't change my life. It's still just . . . a story. I need to have my own moment, one no other person can make happen for me."—J. W., BALTIMORE

"It seems to me that 'traditional' Christians are all about rules and regulations, not spirituality. If you murder someone, but you believe in God and ask for forgiveness, you can be accepted into God's family. However, if you give all of yourself, belongings, money, and material things to better someone's life and/or the world around you, but believe in God as a spiritual energy rather than as a man named Jesus who once walked around on earth, you're going straight to hell. How is that supposed to make sense?" —L. B, BELLEVUE., WA

Talk Amongst Yourselves

What do you think about the premise that it's simply not possible for a person to constantly be filled with the Holy Spirit?

Do you think it's just part of being human that there will always be within you something that vigorously resists God's unqualified love for you? What do you think God's relationship is to that quality within you?

In what ways if any do you think you ever expect—or at least act like you expect—Jesus to bear more of the responsibility than you for the relationship you have with him?

What do you think about the relationship between "secular" psychology and Christianity? Do you think Christ really *is* the only shrink anyone ever needs, or do you think we sometimes have psychological problems that are so unique to us that solving them does take the kind of in-depth, issue-specific approach we typically associate with psychotherapeutic methodologies?

Don't you think it sounds cool just to *say* "psychotherapeutic methodologies"?

6

Are They Talkin' to Us?
Are They Talkin' to *Us?!*

OKAY. SO LET'S ASSUME that through much prayer, thought, and . . . more prayer and more thought, we've left behind the Isle de' Misfits and arrived on God's Mainland, from which we now feel Absolutely Empowered to get out there and shine our love light on every last one of the lucky Normies in our lives.

Hallelujah! It's time to uncork our divine Love Mojo!

Yippee! Grab some bottled water! We're out of here! Let's go . . . let's call . . . let's swing by the home of . . . let's dash right over to . . .

Wait a minute.

Where *are* all the Normies in our lives?

Oh, that's right: They're all way, way over there, on the other side of The Great Divide.

We don't *have* any Normies in our lives.

Shoot. Don't you hate it when that happens? Don't you hate it when it turns out that you spend so much time being with your fellow Christians that you end up not really having anyone in your life who *isn't* a fellow Christian?

Stupid fellow Christians. If only we all weren't so Totally Rewarding to hang out with.

Well, we are. And that's just too bad, because our Lord (in case you'd by any chance forgotten what this book is about) has commanded us to love our neighbors as we love ourselves. And there's no escaping exactly what that means: We've got to log in some pretty serious time Mingling With The Normies.

And remember: Our mission isn't to just mingle with the Normies, either; our mission is to *love* the Normies. Which—even in this time of Cyber-Rapport—means actually and personally spending real time with them, and really getting to know them.

So let's do this, man.

Let's begin to tear down the wall separating Us from Them.

Now, the main thing to remember about *normies americanus* is that in almost every single way they're exactly like us—except profoundly different. The first big difference between their kind and ours that immediately comes to my mind, for example, is that Normies, by just about any measure, have sex drives that are completely out of control. Doesn't it seem like sex is all those people ever *think* about? It's all over their movies, TV shows, books—they muck up perfectly good *halftime* shows with it; their *dentists* probably strut around in glittering bikini briefs, and keep disco music blaring through their offices.

Really—it's a wonder Normies ever see the light of day at all.

Those poor, poor lost souls. If only they could be more like we Christians. We almost *never* make the object of our wholesome sexual desire anyone but our (opposite-gender!) husband or wife—and even *then* only within the context of procreation, or at the very least of divinely inspired emotional intimacy.

Even now, as I write this, it's ridiculous how much I personally am not thinking about sex. The very idea of harboring any kind of pervy sexual "fantasy" about . . . oh, I don't know . . . say, the woman in the navy blue skirt and white blouse whom yesterday I saw shopping for peaches in the grocery store, is as foreign to me as a steaming bowl of monkey brains for dinner.

Seriously. Monkey brains.

I mean, c'mon.

Hefting and squeezing peaches.

I'm so sure.

But that's enough about me; this is about Normies, and how utterly different they are from you and me. And it is of course the nature of the differences between us and them that we must now seek to understand. We want to know what makes Normies tick—what gets them out of bed each morning, what revs them up and keeps them moving ahead moment after moment, and day after day.

What we want to know is who—oh, *who?*—*are* the Normies, really?

And I believe that we can narrow our interests down to something even more unambiguous than that. Because I think that ultimately the truly fascinating question about the Normies doesn't have as much to do with who *they* really are, as it does about what they really think about us.

It's like that old joke, "But enough about me: What do *you* think of me?" Funny, yes. But, like so many jokes, what makes it funny is that it's something we really would say if we were drunk.

And even though we're not drunk (well, *I'm* not), in this case it *is* a reasonable thing for us to ask, because in truth the Big Rock in the shoe of our relationships with Normies is our faith, right? That's really the only difference between us, isn't it? Other than that, everything's good. Everyone's happy. No one's got a problem with anyone else. In fact (let us never, ever forget), if it weren't for our faith, we'd *be* Normies.

But we're not. We're separate from them.

And what separates us from them is our religion.

So in that sense, Christianity is a very real problem.

It's not a problem for *us*, of course. We're down with the Lord like a wood cord in a Ford. We know how *we* feel about our faith — about the thing that in so many ways keeps us from the Normies. What we're maybe less sure of, though, is how *they* feel about our faith — or why they feel whatever ways they might about it. And it is not enough for us to simply say, "Well, they just don't believe," and leave it at that. Normies don't believe in Christianity for very real and specific reasons. They've *learned* not to believe in it. And if we're going to have integrity about the way we perceive, approach, and interact with our nonbelieving brothers and sisters, then we're going to have to be open to hearing and understanding some of the things about our faith that keep them away from it.

And we've also got to be ready for some of what we'll learn about that to hurt a little bit, because it's a pretty safe bet that just about every Normie out there who'd rather have thistles jammed up their nose than even consider becoming a Christian feels that way not so much because of whatever they've learned about our religion in any kind of direct or firsthand fashion, but more because of the impression *we* have made upon them.

Normies don't stay away from Christianity because they *love* to sin so much that they just can't imagine ever having to feel guilty over anything crude or mean-spirited that they ever do.

They don't stay away because they just can't imagine a benevolent, all-powerful creator of the universe.

They don't stay away because they just can't imagine cleaving to a set of fixed moral prescriptions.

They don't even stay away because they just can't imagine actually having to be anywhere besides in bed on Sunday mornings.

Nah — it's too easy to assume that kind of stuff.

Normies stay away from Christianity because of us.

Us! Can you imagine? *Us!*

It's the very definition of incomprehensible.

Haven't they ever tasted our homemade cupcakes (or our *donuts*)? Have they ever even *tried* to get invited to one of our barbeque parties?

Have they never heard how well so many of us sing?

Clearly, we're going to need a little more information if we're going to clear up this complete mystery as to why anyone would want to avoid being around us.

Although that doesn't sound like a particularly inviting conversation, does it? Who wants to hear what someone *doesn't* like about them? I sure don't. I've been happily married to the same (extraordinary) woman for over twenty-five years, and if she so much as vaguely hints at the idea that I, say, stop trying to whistle at the same time I'm chewing food, it's all I can do not to immediately start attacking her *and* pouting. It's just hard for any of us to ever hear anything negative about ourselves.

Yet healing a broken relationship in our lives means attentively listening to what the person estranged from us has to say about us or the problem between us. Until I was thirty-eight, I was about as estranged from Christians as a person can get, and it's through both being a Normie and knowing so many other Normies in my life (I've moved around a *lot*—and, weirdly enough, have had some forty different full-time jobs) that I'm more familiar than at this point I'd prefer to be with the key reasons so many Normies don't like (us) Christians. And as a Christian, I really do think it's important that we hear some of those reasons. Sure, doing so will hurt; we're bound to respond to some of the Normies' gripes against us with defensiveness and even anger. But if we just hang in there, and allow ourselves to hear how at least some Normies perceive us, then when the smoke between our two camps has cleared, at the very least we'll have a better understanding of where exactly we stand in relationship to so many of those whom the Lord (whether we like it or not) has sent us to love.

We can't go meet someone if we don't know where they are, eh?

So let's find out where they are! What the heck! Christians are *nothing* if not resilient, right? And you and I both know that Normies don't know us anywhere near as well as they think they do. And that's perfectly fine; that's something we can change. But before we begin that business, let's first take a deep breath, and face what Normies do, in fact, think of us. And let's do so in a form that shows that, despite what *some* might think, we Christians really *are* the hippest thing since double-shot soy lattes with extra foam and cinnamon on top.

The Top 10 Reasons Normies Don't Like Us

Reason # 10: *They think we're emotionally stunted.*

Stupid butthead Normies. They tend to think that we view the world entirely in blacks and whites, that we lack a fundamental comprehension of all of those emotional realities that are, essentially, gray — or that are at least open to contextual modifications. Hearing us say, for instance, "I simply can't imagine how any woman could ever prostitute herself," leads them to conclude that we lack the emotional complexity to understand how likely it is that we would, in fact, prostitute ourselves, if ever we found ourselves in the kinds of conditions that sometimes leave people no choice but to do those sorts of things. They think that because (we think) that we already *know* how we would feel and act in every imaginable situation, the rich subtlety, complex beauty, and exquisitely sweet pain of everyone *else's* emotional life is largely lost upon us. In a word, they think that many of us lack (of all things) empathy.

Reason #9: *They think we're intellectually immature.*

Normies think that we can't think—and they think that because they think that we think that we already know the answers to all of the questions that keep so many of *them* thinking so hard. (Ha! Let one of *them* come up with a sentence like that!) How did the world begin? What exactly is evil? How probable is it that there's life on other planets? What happens to us after we die? How do we really *know* what's right and wrong? How in the world did the hairless *mole* ever come about? For just about any question that's really worth asking, Christians (thank God!) already have an answer. To Normies, though, a lot of those answers seem laughably untenable. A virgin gets "mysteriously" pregnant. A whale swallows a guy for three days, and then hairballs him out whole. Adam's missing rib transforms into someone who was (well, certainly at *first*) totally worth the trade. Jesus turns a few fish into an al fresco meal for thousands. It all sounds so intellectually ... undemanding. The short of it is that Normies believe that we've traded the security of having all the answers for that part of our brain that's *supposed* to rationally analyze and evaluate those answers. (They also think that what information we do take in comes only from Christian media; they think that we only consider ideas that have been church-sanctioned. At least, I think that's what they think. I'll check with my pastor, to be sure.)

Reason #8: *They think we're at war with our sexuality.*

Normies believe that Christians are basically crazy about anything having to do with sex. They think our whole thing with gender *generally* is a little, shall we say, outmoded—not to say outright chauvinistic. Knowing that the Bible tells us that men are to be the head of the household, for instance, leads Normies to conclude that within her household a Christian mom's status must fall somewhere above pets and children, but below having anything at all to say about who has to make dinner *again.*

Normies know that we (or that at least most of us) think that sex outside of marriage is a sin. (They also think that we're not too thrilled about sex *inside* of marriage, unless while we're having it there's a "What to Name Your Baby" book on the nightstand beside us.) Normies think that by hating sex so much, we hate one of the most fundamentally delightful things about being human. They think it means we hate a huge part of ourselves. And they think it means that we think that because of what *they* think about sex, they're hedonistic animals with few if any moral bearings.

In short, Normies feel that their natural fun and joy is grist for our unnatural condemnation of them.

Reason #7: *They think we're absurdly conceited and smug.*

Every Normie knows that every one of we Christians believes a few Totally Key things about ourselves: That we have a close and personal relationship with God Almighty; that after we die we're going to spend eternity in paradise; and that no matter what terrible things we do, God will always forgive us our transgressions. Not (let's face it) unreasonably, Normies feel that believing these things about ourselves gives us just about every last reason in the world to feel (and so to naturally act) as if our lives, character, and experience is simply of a higher order than is anyone's who doesn't claim those three things for themselves.

Reason #6: *They think we're hypocrites.*

We've all heard this one before: We sin on Saturday; we're forgiven on Sunday. We say we're all about love; yet we've used the Bible to justify such atrocities as slavery, the Inquisition, our long and shameful history of anti-Semitism, and not exactly returning the favor when the Indians welcomed us to the New World. We say we believe in giving to the poor; we hoard riches for ourselves. And just about everywhere Normies look, they see another news story about our corrupt televangelists, our profligate pastors, our child-molesting priests, our overzealous and even violent fanatics.

Man. These reasons Normies don't like us really *are* troubling to delineate.

I think it's time for a little comic relief, don't you?

Okay, so why do ducks have webbed feet?

For stomping out fires.

I only know exactly one joke, and that's it.

Funny joke, or something stupid that doesn't even make sense?! *You be the judge!*

If perchance you like that joke, then you'll probably chuckle heartily at its companion, which is this: Why do elephants have webbed feet? *To stomp out burning ducks.*

Hilarious follow-up joke, or so confusingly lame you're thinking about dropping this book into the gutter?! Let *me* be the judge!

I'm voting it's funny.

Plus, littering is bad.

Besides: Ducks putting out fires with their feet! Panicked elephants stomping burning ducks! *Totally funny!*

Um. Or not.

Speaking of stuff that's not funny at all, let's get back to the Job at Hand, shall we?

Reason #5: *They think we're emotionally unavailable.*

Boy, you try to alleviate a little stress with some perfectly innocent ducks-a'fire humor, and the next thing you know you're "emotionally unavailable."

Stupid Normies, with their touchy-feely "relating," and their hot oil massages, and their . . . *psychology* classes. It's all you can do to pry those bleeding hearts *off* one another.

No, but to many Normies, we Christians seem so intent upon coming across as being One with God that basically we end up refusing to act human; they think that our ceaseless determination to seem angelic means that we never allow ourselves to be emotionally vulnerable, or to in any way reveal our insecurities. They think we'd rather do just about anything than admit that we're still in any way struggling to improve ourselves.

Reason #4: *They think we're desperate to convert them.*

It's pretty difficult for Normies to think that Christians are capable of ever seeing them as anything other than Conversion Fodder. They know that converting unbelievers is a humongous part of our life's mission.

They know that, when it comes to them, we most definitely have an agenda. And they don't exactly see that as a "Welcome!" mat.

Reason #3: *They think we're fanatics.*

Normies know that we firmly believe—that in fact it's fundamental to everything we believe—that no religion is as valid as Christianity, that no other religion is *true.* That conviction works for us, of course—but it sure doesn't for them. From the Normies' point of view, our insistence that our God is the only real God, and that our way is the only way to *get* to the only real God, can hardly help but make us seem like . . . well, dogmatic zealots. Normies tend to believe that there is much to recommend and respect in each of the world's major religious traditions. They believe that tolerance is a sign of kindness and respect, and that our particular brand of intolerance is a sign that, at heart, the only people we *really* mean well are those who believe exactly what we do. Not so good. And particularly unhelpful in these most troubling of times, when, let's face it, Normies have all the reason they need to attribute so much of what's wrong in the world today to religious fundamentalism.

Reason #2: *They think we dress like dorks.*

Why is a mystery. At this very moment, for instance, I am wearing a short-sleeved button-collar Madras shirt tucked into ironed white shorts, with black socks and sandals. I look cool *and* hot. And yet I know that if, dressed as I am, I were to stroll into my local Internet café, Wired &Wireless (or whatever it's called), I'd elicit sundry surreptitious slacker-snickers. (Quick: Say it three times. Or *once,* even.) Like *those* fashion victims know so much about what looks great, with their scruffy jeans, and their black T-shirts, and their . . . scary jewelry.

Oh, but that we could all live in a world where nobody cared about "fashion statements" at all!

Well, there are many things in our lives that need doing.

And we'll just have to accept that one of them is getting everyone to dress right.

And the number one reason Normies don't like us is . . .

THEY KNOW WE DON'T RESPECT THEM!

Ta-da!

That's it.

That's the whole deal, right there. *That's* what's at the core of our deep and constant disconnect from non-Christians; that's the mother seed from which just about all nine of the funky fruits above sprout.

I think the fact that nonbelievers are 100 percent positive that we don't respect them is the most pervasive, corrosive, and least considered aspect of the everyday, common relationship between Christians and non-Christians. I'm convinced it's *why* there's such a rift between Christians and non-Christians.

Back before I was a Christian, I used to hate talking to Christians, since the one thing about them of which I could always be sure was that they did not, and could not, respect me. They might *like* me; I'm a funny guy: Many people, of varying faiths and persuasions, find my squirting lapel flower pretty darn amusing before they start punching me. But I can definitely tell you that, yuks or no, it basically bites to be a non-Christian talking to a Christian. Because who likes to be in a conversation with someone whom they *know* thinks that when it comes to every single last thing in life that matters at *all*, they're as wrong as five when the question is what's two plus two. It's just not a good basis upon which to build a mutually rewarding conversation — let alone a relationship. It means that a typical conversation between a Christian and a non-Christian can't ever *go* anywhere; it's dead before it's begun.

Here — let me show you what, when I wasn't a Christian, used to always shoot through my brain whenever I was talking to someone who was. If at a party, say, I discovered via Happy Party Small Talk that the person with whom I was chatting was a Christian, the text of my internal mental response, slowed down and transcribed, would read about like this:

"Oh no. A Christian. Well, that explains the outfit. And now I'm so bored I'd give anything if my lapel flower hadn't run out of water. I shouldn't have chased that one lady around with it. Man, could she *move* in those heels. A Christian! Why does this always happen to me? What is it about me that attracts Christians like bugs to a bug light? They must pick up on some kind of Total

Sinner vibes I put off. They *sense* my presence. At their churches, in secret, at night, their leaders implant in their heads electronic Pagan Detection Alert systems (PDAs!), which, when they're in social situations, the Christians secretly switch on—by, like, pressing a little button implanted in their leg, or tugging on their ear—and then that digitized internal screen pops up inside their eyes, just like Governor Talk Funny's in the Terminator movies. Then I come into their scanning range, and their PDA starts beeping and carrying on so much they have to figure out a way to nonchalantly muffle their eyeballs. And then—while they're pressing a napkin to their eyes, or pretending to sneeze into a couch cushion—their PDAs pop my classification onto their internal screen: 'Category Five: SACRIFICES CATS! SACRIFICES CATS!'

"Actually, this Christian seems pretty nice. They usually do—same as everyone does during the Intro Phase of interacting. Too bad the Batmobile of any conversation I could ever have with a Christian necessarily blows four tires before it can even get on the road. This person right here, for instance, couldn't care less about who I am; what they *care* about is who they might be able to turn me into. Drag. We can't get to know each other at all—because once this person finds out I'm not a Christian, then as far as they're concerned they're going to already know everything about me: At that point, it's not possible for me to be anything at all to them other than a Wrong Way Corrigan. It's so obnoxious, to be so categorically shut down that way. And it's such a drag for them, too—whether they know it or not. Because it means that whenever a Christian meets anyone new, they go into that interaction totally lacking the one thing that makes it so exciting for everyone else in the world to meet new people: that thrilling, delightful feeling people get whenever they realize that a new acquaintance is actually interesting—that they're funny, or smart, or have done fascinating things, or look at life in some way that's unique or engaging, that they're actually worth *respecting*. Feeling that way about someone you've just met—or even just thinking you *might* feel that way about someone you've just met—is one of the best feelings in life. It's so fun to be talking to someone, and think, 'Wow! This person really seems to *rock!*' And then you become deeply curious about that person, and look forward to getting to know them better. That's such a marvelous, exciting process! It's why people *have* parties. It's sooooo what people love to do!

"Unless they're Christians. Then that entire emotional experience is utterly foreign to them. Tragically, Christians can't *have* that Party Hearty experience, because they're incapable of truly *being* curious about what makes another person tick. All they *can* care about is whether or not the person they're talking to is Christian. If it turns out that their new acquaintance is Christian, then they already know what makes that person tick; if it turns out they're not, then there's nothing *left* about that person to render them worthy of truly enthusiastic curiosity.

"It's, like, 'Oh, you're a Christian? Me too! Hallelujah! Well, this is boring, since we already know everything about each other. Let's go find some people who aren't saved, and try to save them.' Or it's 'Oh, you're not a Christian? Then you're *absolutely wrong.*' Either way, the buzzy, natural energy that exists between two compatible people who've just met is completely missing—which is why 'Christian Party' and 'So Boring You Want To Slit Your Wrists With A Punch Glass' are synonymous.

"The Christian's faith, to the Christian, negates the validity of the non-Christian's reality. A Christian simply cannot see a non-Christian as an equal.

"What a massively freakin' drag.

"Oh, well. You can't save a Christian. And God help the person who's sure they already know everything: It means they've stopped learning, which is a special hell all its own. Hey! The crab cakes are almost gone!"

And that's what pretty much always shot through the head of Pre-Christian Me whenever I met one of . . . us.

Except, you know, a *lot* faster—and (of course) all at once. In real time the above would have just gone: "Oh no, a Christian. *Yawn.* Hey, the crab cakes are almost gone!"

I suppose this goes without saying, but since as far as I can tell you have to say something before it officially qualifies as something you don't have to say, allow me to say this: I'm about as normal a human as you'll ever find. I just don't have the energy, or the background, or the . . . natural wiring, or whatever, to be in any particular way odd or eccentric. I love the TV show *Friends.* I think *Seinfeld* is hilarious. I find the enjoyment of either greatly enhanced via the magnificent miracle of microwaveable popcorn. I've rented so many movies from Blockbuster I'm surprised it's not called Shorebuster. I wish my dad showed me more affection. I wish I were better looking. I love my wife. I worry about not being any richer as I get older.

I'm just . . . normal. And while that's not exactly something I go around bragging about, it does mean that if the above was my Insta-Response to meeting a Christian, it's a safe bet that it's also the response of about eighteen quadrillion other Normies whenever they meet a Christian.

Normies think Christians don't respect them.

And though it pains me to say it, I think they're right.

Ouch

"People's faith in what's beyond this life takes many, many different forms. We should all respect those differences, and resist the temptation to become zealots for whatever form of faith we personally think is best. Failing to do that is the one sure way for our own faith to eventually lose its true meaning."—M. M., CHICAGO

"I feel that many Christians are deluded about how to best spread their message. It's simply annoying to have someone tell you what to think or believe. It seems to me that when Jesus said, 'You are the light of world,' he was saying to be the light, to be a living example of a whole human. Christians should spend less time talking about what they believe, and more time *showing* what they believe. That is how conviction works. I see many Christians who preach the word, but who then treat others with little respect. The Christian emphasis needs to fall back to human compassion, not the need to be right."—T. S., SUMMIT COUNTY, OH

"I love Christians who have ethics and values, but as a Jew, I hate the way some (emphasis *some)* try to convert Jews. While they certainly have a first amendment right to try doing that, I wish they'd take a step back and see how disrespectful it is to others. They'd be much better off if they'd just try to set a good example, and leave the converting to God."—C. O., OMAHA

"Whenever I'm approached by someone trying to convert me, I can't help but feel that that person is showing an incredible lack of respect for me, my religion, and my ability to choose a faith for myself. Religion is a choice you make for yourself. Anyone who tries to make that decision for you must think they are better or smarter than you. Above all, what we need in the dynamic between

Christians and non-Christians is more respect."—R. E., DALLAS

Talk Amongst Yourselves

As a Christian, what's the closest relationship you've ever had with a non-Christian? What was it about that person that you liked so much? How big of a deal was it that the two of you didn't share the same religion?

Is there any possible way you can think of for a non-Christian to feel as if a Christian *fully* respects them, when they know the Christian believes that they're tragically wrong in choosing not to be Christian?

Is it possible for a Christian to communicate full respect and love (as opposed to either alone) to a non-Christian, without in any way compromising his or her love and devotion to Christ?

Do you think that by virtue of being a Christian you in any way miss out on some or even a lot of good, fun, healthy stuff in life? Why or why not?

What is it about ducks that's so funny? Is it their feet? Their beaks? Their whole ducky attitude? What?

7

So "Luckier" *Isn't* the Same as "Better"?

AS I SAY, I'M certainly aware of how intrinsically repellent it is to assert that Normies are correct when they think we don't respect them. Like you, I'm deeply aware that if Christ's dying on the cross did anything for us, it made us humble.

But I'm also aware that another effect of Christ's dying for us *personally* is that it's pretty much guaranteed to leave us Christians, in our heart of hearts, feeling like we really *are* better than someone who hasn't professed Jesus Christ as their personal Lord and savior.

And it gets worse! Not only do we Christians believe that we're fundamentally (so to speak) superior to Normies, but there's no possible way that we can *help* thinking that, either.

No.

Possible.

Way.

On.

Mars.

I.

Mean.

Earth. (Okay, fine: I'll be suggesting a way 'ere long. But it's *practically* impossible.)

And it's not like Normies don't know we feel this way. *We*

might have trouble coming to terms with anyone thinking that, in the high school of life, we're the conceited, cliquish cheerleaders just *basking* in the allure of our radiant cuteness, but, to a Normie, saying, "Christians think they're superior" is like saying, "Beavers have big teeth," or "Smoking crack is bad for you."

It's, like — duh.

And if we think that there's anything slightly unreasonable or unfair about the Normies' certainty that we hold ourselves to be much better than they, then it's possible that we need to think about the idea that we might not be thinking enough about some of the most basic components of our belief system, nor about the natural ramifications of those components.

You know what I'm talkin''bout. You know where this is going. You already see what's starin' at us all like a big fat "WANTED!" poster featuring our grim visage. You understand that if person A believes that they're dead-on right about every single last thing that's critical to the human mind, body, and soul, and that person B is absolutely *wrong* about those exact same things, then it's just about impossible for person A not to feel plain ol' fashioned *better* than person B: mentally healthier, closer to the truth, better prepared to deal with all of life's big issues ... just *better*, relative to what most people would agree are the most important matters in life.

And if person A says that they *don't* feel like they're fundamentally superior to person B, then person A is either lying, or seriously out of touch with a whole bunch of their inner reality. Neither's good.

And the thing about our feeling superior to nonbelievers is that we *have* to feel that way. We could no sooner help feeling that way than we could help feeling wet in a running shower, or anxious when our dentist leans over us with a whining drill in his grip. The constant, abiding sense that we've got it all *over* Normies is to our belief system what wrapping paper is to a Christmas gift: It's just part of the package. It's who we are. You put a giant next to a dwarf, and the giant *is* gonna feel taller. He can't help it. He looks down; he feels taller. It comes with the view.

I mean, we're close to *God*. That's pretty much the headiest stuff in the universe. It's not like we're close to the head of our local library, or to the chef behind the counter at Pierre's Bistro and Take-Out. It's not like Beefy the Door Master thinks we're hot and always lets us right inside Club Cool. We're talking about being on close and intimate terms with *God*. I mean, talk about being on the "A" list.

God! We're close to *God!* The creator and sustainer of All That Is! The supreme power of the universe! The Alpha and Omega! The end all and be all of Mr. Bigs!

And God *chose* us to be that way, too. God chose us to be so close to him that he's actually *in* us all the time!

He likes us! He really, really likes us!

As Christians, we belong to God Almighty, and no other.

Now in what world does that fact leave us feeling like we're morally or spiritually equal (let alone—perish the thought!— *inferior*) to someone who at *best* belongs to a gym, or to Wine of the Month Club, or whatever? In no world at all, that's where. And *certainly* not in this one. That's just not the system we're in. That's not how things operate here on planet Earth. We can cry humility and universal love, and claim for ourselves whatever noble attitudes or beliefs we want to, but it won't change the bottom-line fact that, for the here and now, we're as human as humans get.

And humans, by nature, identify, respond to, and participate in Natural Hierarchies via an instinct they can no sooner shut off than they can the ones that make them preen to be attractive or jump when something goes bump in their night.

We can't help it, man.

At heart, we're all Darwinians.

Yikes.

Moving right along: The point is, that one of the things that all people very naturally tend to do is rate themselves in relationship to others. It would (perhaps) be great if we *didn't* do that—and of course we very often rise above doing that—but sometimes, like it or not (and *think* about it or not), we *do* do that. And there's no sin in it; it's simply a function of being the Highly Sociable Creatures we are. We couldn't have brains and *not* have them automatically rate things—and especially not have them rate the very thing they most care about, which (bless their busy little synapses) is the Entire Identity to which they are inextricably bound.

Think about your life: You have always rated yourself in relationship to others—and you always will. And for any of us to try to pretend like we personally *don't* do that—like we're somehow so evolved spiritually that that kind of thinking is simply beneath us—is (besides smacking of the very sort of conceit that we surely want no part of) like trying to pretend as if we wouldn't care one whit if we came home one night after a huge, sensational party and discovered that for the entire night we'd been sporting the shiny skin of a black bean on one of our two front teeth.

We care. We'd mini-*heart attack* care. We'd care about that because we're *all* about who we are in relationship to others.

One's a worker; one's a boss; one guy's won; one guy's lost.

Like it or not, that's . . . the game we play.

And frankly, when it comes to non-Christians, we win The Big Game like Michael Jordan playing one-on-one with Porky the Pig. (Wait: Didn't he actually *do* that in a movie?)

Point is: It's just no contest. How could it be? It's the God of the Christians versus . . . what? Starbucks? The curly fries at TGIF?

Dogs who look cute in sweaters?

Normies have got nothing, basically.

While we have everything.

Hmm.

Nothing, versus Everything.

Not exactly the kind of odds that keep Vegas in business.

So it's obvious enough that in this life we're miles ahead of the Normies. And it's *after* we die that our lead really kicks in! That's when we go to heaven—the greatest place *ever*. For us, the eternal afterlife will be nothing but sheer bliss. But for the poor Normies, the eternal afterlife will be nothing but the feeling of being forever suspended in boiling oil.

And that's it. That's the Enchilada de la Whole. We have God and heaven; Normies have no God (or, much worse, the *wrong* god), and hell.

We win!

They lose!

We make the right choices!

They make the wrong choices!

We're living righteous lives!

They're living sinful lives!

They don't please God!

We *do* please God!

DAD LIKES US BEST!!

Okay? So we're superior; we know we're superior; we (naturally! it's no sin!) feel superior; Normies *know* we feel superior; they know *why* we feel superior; it's because we feel superior that Normies tend not to enjoy hanging around with us.

I mean, Normies might not worship in a church every Sunday,

but they're not *stupid*. They understand the basics of our faith. They know that we think that we're saved, and that they're lost. They're pretty clear on the meaning of the words "saved" and "lost." They know which one it's better to be. They understand why it's inherent in our religion to feel superior to them; they know we could no sooner *not* feel that way than a lion could not feel like he can get a drink from any watering hole on the veldt just about any dang-blangit time he feels like it.

And I know I'm banging on this stuff awfully hard, but it's because I so desperately want *us* to know it, too. I want us to be honest with ourselves and everyone else in the world, and just admit that being a Christian has (naturally!) made us feel superior to those who aren't. There's no way around that simple fact of our human lives. And if we have felt superior to the Normies, then as sure as muck trails a snail we have *acted* superior to the Normies.

And that is why the Normies keep as far away from us as . . . well, as they do.

And that is why we're failing to fulfill Jesus' Great Commandment.

And that is a terrible, terrible thing.

It is broken; and we *do* need to fix it.

So let's.

How We Christians Can Stop Feeling and Acting Superior to Our Nonbelieving Brothers and Sisters

The easy way for us to rid ourselves of whatever sanctimonious self-importance may have attached itself to us is by simply (and constantly) remembering that we're not better than nonbelievers. What we are is *luckier* than nonbelievers. We didn't do anything to get saved. We didn't deserve it. It's not like God was holding auditions for an open spot in heaven, and we just so wowed him with our killer rendition of "Oklahoma!" or "Go Tell It on the Mountain" that we *won*.

Being close to God is something to be grateful for, not proud of.

And that God saves us through no effort of our own is hardly a surprise to we Protestants, eh? If there's *anything* we know, it's that we are saved by the grace of God, and by that alone. That's the single shape of brick from which we build our entire home. That's how we live. That's who we are.

If we Christians know *nothing* else, we know that being arrogant — much less being arrogant about our relationship to God — is about the last thing we'd ever want Jesus to catch us being.

And yet all too often there we are, acting like since Jesus himself isn't present, we will *certainly* do in his stead.

Well, some Christians act like that, anyway.

I don't, of course. But some do. *Lots* do. But I don't, because I've chosen to put obeying Christ's Great Commandment ahead of everything else in my life.

I'm just . . . better, that way.

God is *especially* pleased with me. I . . . sfKI;;;pwofdkd flfljfdj d MY haANDS I CAN'T AOSLS MOVE MYH ANDS RIGHT!!1 [[Mmy Fingers!! s ccsx crazy I wtylggmghoiox alos.w!!

Oh. Whew. Here we are. Cool. I can type again.

Much better.

What in the heck was *that* about?

Oh, well. Life's a mystery.

The point is: We Christians really aren't any better than anyone else. For some reason we may never understand, we became a great deal more fortunate than many others — but what sort of fool takes credit for his own blind luck? Being saved should make us insanely humble, not proud. "There but for the grace of God," and all that.

And let us not (ever) forget that the people we consider unlucky don't consider *themselves* unlucky—and not by a long shot, either. Normies *like* their lives. They're content. They're having fun. They're living rich, emotionally rewarding lives. They're not looking in from outside the candy store that is our lives, wondering why we get all the breaks. They think we wouldn't know a break from a pitchfork. They think we're soft-headed *dupes.*

They feel sorry for us—just like we feel sorry for them.

So it all kind of works out.

Kind of.

Well it *can,* anyway.

And here, ultimately, is how: We need to radically change our paradigm relative to how we relate to Normies.

And I mean, radically.

Out with the old, in with the new.

Let's be bold, or let's be blue.

We're out in the cold; it's time for a clue.

What we're selling's been sold; now what do we do? (And you just got a preview of my next book: *Mother Goose Goes to Seminary.*)

Serious business, now: Our Whole Entire Thing Toward Normies has got to stop being "Let's change them!" and start being, "Let's *not* change them!"

Let's not change them.

Let's stop worrying about changing the minds of people who don't want to believe what we believe. Let's stop pushing our religion on people who are perfectly content doing whatever it is that they've chosen to do, who are happy to travel down whatever course they've chosen for themselves.

Let's really respect people, instead of just *saying* that we respect them.

Let's respect people; let's love people; let's let people be.

It's like Sting said: "I can make love for eighteen hours straight."

No, I mean: "If you love someone, set them free."

Right on, Bee Boy! That's exactly right: It's time to set the Normies free. And I mean really, truly, absolutely free. In our hearts, minds, and souls, it's got to be perfectly okay for non-Christians to *be* non-Christian.

That's it. That's the singular, whole point of this book: It's got to be perfectly okay with Christians if other people aren't Christian.

It works practically (they're not listening anyway); it works emotionally (finally, we can quit stressing over this relentless pressure to convert others); it works theologically (it allows us to fulfill the Great Commandment).

It's time. We've preached enough to people who don't want to hear it. It's time to give them, and us, a break.

It's time to lose the 'tude, dude.

And, lest we forget, it's not like I'm suggesting we give up something that's just working so great for us it'd be a real shame to lose it. We've got to remember that trying to convert people *doesn't work anyway.* I have never known one single person who succeeded in converting a nonbeliever. Not *one.* And I'll bet dollars-to-donuts (so to speak) that you haven't, either. Because trying to change the mind of someone who knows their own mind is like trying to get a fish to climb a tree: It's an effort that's destined to flop. (And, again: We're talking here only about our trying to convert Normies who have never expressed to us any more interest in hearing about Jesus than they have in hearing about Martin Van Buren's haberdasher. If by some [true] miracle we just happen to be there at the time in a Normie's life when he or she is *looking* to get saved—when [glory to God!] they're in some clear way *asking* to be delivered—then we may very well end up being That Day's

Usher. But if the Normie at hand *isn't* having that day or moment, then it's time for us to stop trying to force them to have it.)

It's time we stopped worrying so much about the Great Commission, and started worrying whole oodles more about the Great Commandment.

And let us take great emotional and intellectual care, by the way, *not* to automatically transmogrify, "Love your neighbor as you love yourself" into "Love your neighbor because purely loving someone is the very best way to get them to convert."

That is not what this is about. This is not about loving and accepting people so that they'll eventually convert!

I get that all the time. Very often when I share this "Live and Let Live" idea with a fellow believer, they'll respond with, "Yeah! We *should* love and accept people, just the way they are! *That's* the way to bring people to the Lord!"

And then I have to . . . squirt them again with my flower.

Because that's sooooo not it. Because that's *still* about trying to turn Normies into Christians. And trying to convert nonbelievers is *always* the poison pellet that ruins the water we're serving. Because it *always* means that we think we have something that the nonbeliever is in sore need of. And that *always* means that we think we're in a very critical way better than they. And no matter how charming and humble we think we're being, we will *always* communicate that, in one way or another. And the nonbelievers will *always* recoil from us the second they understand that we're condescending to them and/or trying to emotionally manipulate them.

And everyone always knows when that's happening to them.

And that's why our burgeoning relationships with stranger Normies always (or at least so often) ends up croaking like Kermit under a passing truck.

I'm totally down with becoming, ala Paul in 1 Corinthians, all things to all men. I am *not* down with doing that as a means of eventual conversion. It's got to be *all good* that someone's not a Christian. It's got to be *perfectly okay* that they don't think God became a man named Jesus who purposefully had himself beaten and murdered so that they could lead happier lives and afterlives.

Talking to some guy at your job who's not a Christian? It's okay! Woman you met at your pottery class not a Christian? It's perfectly fine! See a girl in a coffee shop picking up a flyer about a class on "Total Cosmic Integration as the Path to Divine Enlightenment"? No problemo!

Worried that if someone you know or love doesn't get saved it means they're going to spend eternity in hell? Well, that's a right and noble sentiment—and it's *too bad for you.* Because even if hell is real (and I mention the "if" only because I know that so many Christians consider The Fiery Pit as more of a metaphor than an actual, genuine place—which will make a terrific conversation some day when you and I really *do* have an eternity to talk), we can't do a dang thing to keep anyone out of hell who doesn't in some very real way *want* to be kept out of hell—which is to say, anyone who doesn't believe in hell in the first place, couldn't care less whether anyone else thinks they're going there or not. As much and as deeply as it pains us, the manifest fact is that we simply cannot convince someone who doesn't believe in Jesus that they're going to burn in hell for that very reason. To a person who isn't Christian, such an assertion sounds the only way it *can* sound: absolutely bonkers (not to mention absurdly uncompassionate). And our sheer fervor for the Normie's ultimate well-being isn't going to help them, either: Believing something with all of our heart doesn't mean anyone else has to even take that belief seriously, much less change their lives around it.

Besides, we don't have to worry that if we don't convert someone, they'll never convert. As nearly impossible as it is for most of us to conceive, the cold truth is that a whole *bunch* of great stuff happens in the world all the time that has nothing whatsoever to do with us.

For example, just yesterday I was amazed to discover that I had absolutely nothing to do with the rescue of two college-age girls whose almost-fun vesselette got lost at sea. Unbelievably, I had to hear about their trauma on the evening news! Can you imagine?! Nobody called me to ask what I thought or wanted to do about those girls being lost at sea. No one rushed over to my place for an emergency consultation. No officials e-mailed me, seeking my advice. Did anyone even *care*, for instance, that I thought the straps used to haul the girls up from the water into the helicopter were *way* too tight? No, they didn't. Forget it. Those girls could have been lifted to safety by their *hair* for all anyone knew that I cared.

The entire rescue operation simply went on without me.

And I guess stuff like that happens *all the time.*

And I suppose that I had better just get used to it.

Because I know that as often and compulsively as I rebel against it, first, foremost, before and ever after, this world belongs to God.

And in God's world, *God* does the things that He wants done. I know I can trust that.

I know that if God wants someone to be saved, that person'll be saved.

It's not up to me.

It was never up to me.

It's *never* about me.

It's about God, and God alone.

God will save whomever he wants to, whenever he wants to, however he wants to.

God *told* us what our number one job is.

And luckily for us (God is good!), that job is so easy that any (and every, actually) dog can do it.

All we have to do is love people with the same unfettered acceptance with which God loves us. And that should hardly be a problem for us: We are, after all, made in God's image. And if God could love us as we were before he saved us (and clearly he did, since he *did* save us), then can't we love Normies just the way *they* are, right now, without trying to do God's job, which is to somewhere in the future either save or Ultimately Judge them? Can't we remember that that *is* God's job, and not ours at all?

I think we can. I think we can love Normies just as we find them, and let God worry about the rest of it.

And loving Normies just as we find them means accepting Normies just as we find them.

And it's through accepting Normies—and only through accepting Normies—that we can come to respect Normies in the same way that we want them to respect us.

God loves, accepts, and respects our sorry butts; we love, accept, and respect the Normies' sorry butts.

And the lives of all of us improve.

It's such a simple, heavenly plan.

Ouch

"Just last week I was cornered by a new acquaintance who wanted to know what church I attend. We had already had a little chat about God telling her to move to Oregon (!), so I didn't think it was an idle inquiry. My first thoughts were: 1. How, where, or if I worship is my own business; 2. Eeek: She's going to want me to go to her church; and 3. She's going to think ill of me because I don't go to church. My religious education is scanty, but I'm pretty sure

Jesus promoted love, tolerance, and turning the other cheek. Things certainly seem to have gone downhill from there. Contemporary Christianity seems to encourage exclusion, judgment, and condemnation. I don't think that's what Jesus had in mind. And I neither understand nor approve of the efforts of Christians, both modern and throughout history, to impose their religious beliefs on others. I feel that the state of my spirituality, much like the state of, say, my checking account, is my business only."—P. K., COLUMBIA CITY, OR

"I am a former 'born again' Christian. It's been my personal experience that Christians treat the poor poorly—much like the Pharisees did in the parable of the old woman with the two coins. I found the church to be political to a fault, and its individual members all too happy to judge and look down on others. As a Christian, my own fervor to witness was beyond healthy. My friends would come to me to vent and express emotions, and all I would do is preach to them. I was of no real comfort to them. I never tried to see anything from their perspective."—J. S. W., PHILADELPHIA

"I'm frequently approached by Christians of many denominations who ask whether I've accepted Christ as my savior. When I have the patience, I politely tell them that I'm Jewish. This only makes them more aggressive; they then treat me like some poor lost waif in need of their particular brand of salvation. They almost act like salespeople working on commission: If they can save my soul, then they're one rung closer to heaven. It's demeaning. I always remain polite, but encounters like these only show disrespect and sometimes outright intolerance for my beliefs and my culture. In Judaism, we do not seek to convert people. That is because we accept that there are many paths to God, and believe that no one religion can lay sole claim to the truth or to God's favor. Each person is free to find his or her own way. To Christians I would say: Practice your religion as you wish. There is no need to try and influence others. If your religion is a true one, people will come to it on their own."—M. S., HONOLULU

"Many of Jesus' teachings were about giving selflessly, but I don't see many Christians actually doing that. Instead of casting off their material possessions and giving them to the poor, they very clearly live for *this* world, and for the betterment of their own situations. Every Christian I've ever known seems to follow the teaching of their 'Lord' halfheartedly, at best."—J. W., SEATTLE

Talk Amongst Yourselves

To what if any extent do you think you're guilty of feeling—at any level, and to whatever degree—superior to non-Christians?

Do you in any way experience as challenging to be both singled out by God to be the beneficiary of his unbounded and unconditional love, *and* to be utterly humble all the time?

Do you think it's possible for a Christian to ever truly accept a non-Christian, just as they are?

Don't you love the phrase, "Being close to God is something to be grateful for, not proud of"? And since this is my book, don't you think that in the interest of marital harmony my wife should be willing to revise her unyielding conviction that it was she, and not I, who thought of it first?

8

Shall We Dance?

SO WHAT WE'RE TALKING about here is learning to see Normies not through our own eyes, but through God's. And when, in the peace of our church's sanctuary or the silence of our own prayer time at home, we give our love to God, and in return feel ourselves filled with God's love for us and all of his creation, we know that that divine view always was, and always will be, the very best view of all.

The problem, of course, is that while giving and receiving the glory of God's love, we tend to close our eyes. Which is great—the view can be *so* splendid when our eyes are closed! God is in his heaven! God is in our hearts! The Normies are beautiful reflections of God's creative light, just like us!

Ahhh. Lovely.

And then we open our eyes again—and slowly but surely our Heavenly Abstracts give way to the concrete, less-than-heavenly aspects of our everyday lives.

God's in his heaven—but our car's in the shop, and was that mechanic actually fighting not to *smile* when he said how much it was going to cost to fix it?

God's in our hearts—but our hearts are pounding like crazy, because we're still crawling along on the freeway at the time we're supposed to be walking into an important meeting at work.

The Normies are beautiful reflections of God's created

light—except can you believe that one girl got a *nose ring?* And have you seen her new boyfriend?! He looks like the centerfold from *Every Mother's Nightmare* magazine!

Stupid concrete, less-than-heavenly aspects of our everyday lives. They're so . . . abrasive. Why—oh, *why?*—must they always intrude upon our lovely ideals with their insipid gnarliness?

Well, they do—and they always have, and they always will. It's all part of God's plan: We're all just angels going through some kind of Earth Boot Camp before we make it into heaven, I guess. Who knows?

All we do know for sure is that we're all in this together, and that God has commanded us to love our neighbors in a *true* way that doesn't make them feel like we secretly wish they were completely different—which is to say in a way that *must* include respecting them, since loving someone without respecting them can't be anything more than condescending to or patronizing them, and who wants to be on either side of that sort of unpleasantness?

Nope. This is about fully Loving and Accepting the Normies.

And, by God, that's just what we're going to do. We're going to move from loving Normies in the abstract whilst thinking and praying about them, to loving and respecting them in real time.

And don't you think we could use seven handy-dandy tips to help us accomplish this goal?

So do I!

Seven Handy-Dandy Tips to Bear in Mind About Any Given Normie When You're Interacting with Them So That It'll Be Easier to Love Them in a Way That Might Not Come So Naturally Once You Find Out They're Pagan Nonbelievers

Tip #1: *Remember Jesus*

Like many others, I find that if ever I'm in the middle of a situation that causes me to feel at any sort of loss, I can regain my sense of purpose and understanding simply by asking myself what Jesus would have done in a similar situation. Of course, Jesus could raise people from the dead and turn water into wine, while I can hardly get out of bed on most mornings, and can barely turn water into coffee. Still, Jesus *is* the ultimate role model. And of all the wondrous, undeniably miraculous things our Lord and Master did while inspiring and freaking people out here on earth, do you know which one *most* impresses me?

Okay, wait—I mean, *besides* when he brought dead people back to life?

Oh—and besides resurrecting himself, of course.

And for sure not counting how he gave sight to that blind guy. Talk about bringing light into the world!

Oh—and how he healed that one lame guy by the pool! That certainly can't be beat.

And of course, who can forget his walking on water? Man. Talk about proving beyond a doubt that you're the Ultimate Lifeguard.

So, I mean, those are all . . . biggies, for sure.

Well anyway, the miracle of Jesus' that I just think completely rocks the universe—the one that I can definitely say most often comes to my own little mind—was his full-on, first-shot-out-of-the-box, Debut Miracle: Turning water into wine.

And why does that particular miracle mean so much to me? I think the answer's obvious: Because of how often I wish I had wine faucets in my house.

I'm kidding, of course. I wish they were *beer* faucets. But that's not the point. The point is that when Jesus first decided to prove that he possessed powers never before seen on this earth, what did he do? *He kicked a party into high gear!*

He didn't turn a gopher into a wooly mammoth. He didn't make trees run around and turn cartwheels. He didn't fly around in the sky, leaving "Repent! I Am God!" written in black smoke behind him.

No.

What he *did*, figuratively speaking, is to pop a little funk on the stereo, and then turn that bad boy up.

He busted out the quality booze at a wedding!

He became nothing less than the all-time, hands down, Ultimate Party Guest.

And his turning water into wine wasn't just some *practice* miracle or anything. It wasn't the result of Jesus being at a wedding and thinking, "Shoot—I forgot to bring a gift. I know! I'll turn these huge barrels of water into wine! Well, maybe not; I'm still not all that good at miracles yet. Yesterday I tried to bring that bird back to life, and all that happened is its feathers fell off. Still, I should be able to handle something as simple as turning water into wine. Water practically *is* wine. Plus, no one even knows I'm at this party; if the miracle flops, I'll just shoot back home. They'll think it was Baal, or Pan, or somebody. And even if the miracle does fail, so what? They'll probably still have water afterward. At worst they'll have grape juice. People love grape juice. As long as I don't turn the water into *sewage* water or anything, I should be all right."

Yeah.

That happened.

What Jesus did that afternoon at that wedding was, to my mind, as powerful a testament to how much he loves people as was his very sacrifice on the cross. I believe that his choosing to make his first miracle turning all that good water into all that good wine says everything any of us will ever need to know about what

Jesus wants our attitude to be toward not just fellow believers, but toward virtually everyone.

It's a pretty safe bet that Jesus fully understands the power of first impressions, don't you think? He knew blessing that wedding with more wine than any of its guests could drink would be recorded as his opening miracle. He knew that for as long as people told his story, they'd remember that *that* was how he first chose to conclusively prove his divinity.

Pretty clearly, he was meaning to tell us something with that choice. And I believe that something was *love people just as you find them.*

He didn't lecture the people at that wedding. He didn't frighten them. He didn't try to convince them of the error of their ways. He didn't start dividing them into groups of good and bad. He didn't *in any way* interfere with what they were doing. He quietly and without fanfare *enhanced* what they were doing—and that was all.

And what were they doing? Dancing, singing, hugging, whooping it up, crying, and in every way acting like people usually do at wedding receptions: Like they're celebrating all the things about being human that deserve to be celebrated.

In a real way that we all understand, there's nothing more gloriously *human* than a wedding reception.

And that's where Jesus decided to launch his ministry.

And that's how: By doing nothing more dramatic than making sure the lovely couple and all their lovely guests didn't run out of wine.

And not that cheap, comes-in-a-gallon-jug wine, either. He gave them good wine. He gave them *great* wine.

Because he wanted them to just keep doing what they were doing when he got there.

I don't see how Jesus could have made any clearer what he

obviously intended to be his first Big Message to anyone who would ever follow him: Accept and love people exactly as they are when you first meet them.

I think he's telling us to just *be* with people.

If we're with someone whose soda is running low, we should ask if we can get them another soda. If their wine glass is empty, we should fetch ourselves a glass, and ask them if they'd like any more. If they're smoking, we should act like we don't mind their smoke blowing on us, and get them an ashtray. If they're eating french fries, we should at least *try* not to steal one when they're looking the other way.

If they're wearing a nose ring, we should tell them it looks cool, and maybe ask them if it hurt them to get it.

When it comes to engaging others — *all* others — we don't have to wonder what Jesus would have done. The Bible's really clear about telling us, over and over again, exactly what he *did* do when engaging others. He loved them. He didn't assess their worth, or evaluate their moral standing, or in any way determine their quality before he loved them. He "simply" loved and respected them, exactly as they were.

Tip #2: *Let Freedom Ring!*

That it's sometimes difficult for us to relate to Normies is because what's at the core of who we are — what defines us — is so different from what's at the core of who they are, right? It's like mixing apples and . . . something you could eat that *didn't* once cause us all to not only get permanently booted from paradise, but to have to actually get jobs. (That's it: I'm permanently boycotting apples, apple pie, and applesauce. From now on, I'm totally drawing the line at Appletinis.)

But what's absolutely worth remembering is that while at our

Spiritual Core we are indeed dramatically different from Normies, in the everyday, practical, *physical* world what mostly distinguishes us from them boils down to nothing more innately disaffecting than that we've given (or at least are forever striving to give) our will over to God, whilst most of them are persisting in the belief that they themselves are Masters of Their Own Destiny.

In a very real sense, we (thank God) have given up trying to win the war that they're still fighting.

They're still out there, standing on their own two feet, believing that *they're* going to discover the answers to all of their questions, and that *they're* going to make themselves content and peaceful, and that *they're* going to figure out how to deliver themselves from their pain.

And we're in a whole different posture — on our knees — waiting for God to take the lead on all those same issues in our lives.

Normies are in the driver's seat of their car, and we're in the passenger seat of ours.

That's it. That's the gist of the big, *practical* difference between us and Normies. Christians know their free will is a gift from God, and non-Christians believe it just *arrives,* along with their toes, body hair, and digestive systems.

And that's not such a dramatic difference, is it? Especially given how often we, too, forget who's really in the driver's seat of our lives? And there's no shame in a person wanting to drive their own car, is there? Surely we can respect people who are depending upon their own strength, free will, and personal resources to get themselves through their every day. Handling life that way is, after all, the most natural thing in the world. It's what people are best equipped to do; more, it's what God *designed* us to do. We are born to be independent — to fight hard, to tackle life's challenges on our own — to believe that, come You Know What or high water, we can and will do whatever it takes to survive, if not outright prevail.

Normies believe that. They believe that they can win.

Well, God bless 'em. If I was God, and I looked down, and I saw someone really *sticking* with their free will, I imagine that I wouldn't be too terribly upset with them at all. At least I'd know they were really *using* the richest, most defining gift I ever gave them or any other human — that they really *believed* in the worth of my most precious bequest to them.

If I was God, I could see that working for me. Kind of. For a while, at least. Then I imagine that I'd start (as, God knows, we all know God does) slowly but very surely persuading people who are depending upon their own will to seriously consider giving *my* will, and *my* way, a shot in their lives. And I think we can trust that that's the kind of transition God is working in the hearts and lives of all nonbelievers. And I think that means that *we* can let go of worrying about what other people are doing with their lives, or how or why they're doing it. I think it means we can appreciate — we can *empathize* — with whatever any given Normie is doing when we meet them, and with however they're doing whatever they're doing. Because we know what they don't: That it's only a matter of time before God, in one way or another, becomes every bit as real to them as we would ever desire him to be.

And remember: It's not even that we have to be okay with any given person *never* becoming a Christian; we just have to be okay with them not becoming Christian during the relatively short period of time in which we know them. That's not that big of a deal. Life is long. God's On The Case. We can relax.

Tip #3: *Guess Who's Coming to Dinner?*

Want to instantly feel respect and love for just about any Normie?

Imagine that that Normie is God's Direct Representative — an Appointed Ambassador, if you will. How do you know that any given person isn't an angel in disguise? Remember those three Mysterious Visitors who came to Abraham's house that one afternoon? The moment they showed up on his tentstep, Abraham became the host with the most — and this was after God had already made it abundantly clear that Abraham was his Number One Human. If anyone ever had a right to go "Holier Than Thou" on other people, it was Abraham.

And yet there he was, practically groveling to serve some (truly, as it turns out) perfect strangers.

And yeah, Abraham may have sensed that his three guests weren't exactly Moe, Larry, and Curly Bedouin. He might have suspected that he was dealing with the Lord. But he wasn't *positive* that he was. And it's clear enough it wouldn't have mattered: You can tell he treated everyone with the same sincere and spontaneous graciousness with which he treated those three.

Hebrews 13:2 says, "Do not forget to entertain strangers, for by so doing some people have entertained angels without knowing it."

And there's the lesson, staring us right in the face: Every single one of us should learn to tap dance or juggle. Perhaps a magic trick or two. *Something* entertaining.

No, but the bottom line is that none of us knows when or how (exactly) the Lord is going to return, or what angels he might first send out to scout about in advance. So we'd do well to treat everyone as if they *were* those angels. That's what Abraham did — and it turned out that one time he was *right*. If reflexive humility and respect for others was good enough for the Father of the Faithful, it's good enough for us to aspire to whenever we're faced with anyone who *seems* to be just another nonbelieving, noodle-headed Normie. Think how many people thought the *first* time around that Jesus was just some lowlife hammer-monkey in need of a haircut and a shave. When he comes back, do *you* want to risk being the lunkhead who, to whatever degree, *condescended* to him or his advance emissaries?

And the best part of treating everyone as if they're essentially Jesus in disguise is that when we look for the divine in someone, there's just no way to miss it.

Tip #4: *They Are Heroes Among Us*

There are millions of Normies out in the world who have dedi-cated their lives to doing what amounts to God's work. Teachers, policemen, doctors, nurses, firemen, social workers, rescue workers, military personnel—there are all kinds of Normies who spend every day working their tails off to make the world a genuinely better place for us all. And even if any given Normie isn't, in the way of a fireman or a cop, a hero for a living, it's a safe bet that in their lives he or she has shown remarkable courage, or phenomenal perseverance, or has deeply sacrificed for another. I think it's a good idea for each one of us Christians to every once in a while take a moment to remember that our lives are filled with people who may not share our religious beliefs, but who are, by any definition, heroes.

Tip #5: *They've Got Skills*

If there's one thing we can depend upon being true about virtu-ally any Normie, it's that they possess talents and abilities that can make us look like a trained seal's beachball. If the marvelous, prac-tically freakish way in which God gifted the Normie with whom we're dealing isn't immediately obvious to us, we can trust that it's only because we don't yet know that person well enough. But it's a certainty that sooner or later, in one way or another, that person will, in some way, blow us out of the water. It might be the way they

SHALL WE DANCE? 127

sing. It might be the special way they have with animals—or with children, or the elderly, or the disabled. It might be the way they intuitively perceive patterns of colors and lines around them. It might be that they can read a book in about the same amount of time it takes us to read a billboard. But it's going to be *something*. Every single human being on this planet is truly and uniquely spectacular. That singular, indelible miracle is God's very trademark.

Tip #6: *They Love Pizza*

If there's one thing we can say about Normies, it's that they love pizza. Back when I was a Normie, I loved pizza so much that during a time when I ended up *working* in a pizza place, I *still* loved pizza. Even after being a *slave* to pizzas all day, I used to have my friends call in bogus orders about fifteen minutes before we closed, because *we got to take home pizza that loser customers ordered but then never picked up.*

It was wrong, to have my friends call in fake orders so that they and I could then gorge on a huge free pizza. But let's face it: That's what pagan, heathen, working-overtime-for-free teenagers do.

Wrong, wrong, wrong. I can only hope that my old Purloin-A-Pizza pagan pals have since been saved (lest they end up in the biggest Pizza Oven of all!).

Now that I personally am no longer a poor pagan purposefully purloining piping-hot pepperoni pizzas, I find that, as a Christian, I *still* love pizza. Becoming a Christian didn't change that.

So much of who we are—so much of what we experience—has nothing whatsoever to do with our religion. Before going into Chow Mode, we Christians may say grace, and the Normies may not—but once munching has commenced, we're all the same.

And if we're all eating pizza, we're *really* all the same.

Religion mainly happens on the spiritual plane; our lives — the lives of *all* of us — mainly happen on the physical. If the spiritual's going to be any kind of obstacle in the way of our happily relating to another person, then while we're with that person let's just put our religion on the back burner. It'll be okay there; it'll wait. Surely there's enough about life down here on earth that we have in common with the Normies to allow for our bonding with any one of them for a good, long time. What separates us can wait.

Tip #7: *Pray*

Pray, pray, pray. Ask God for insight and wisdom relative to your relationship with Normies. *Beg* God to help you please him. Pray to him to open your heart, and to show you how to love nonbelievers in the way you'd want him to love you if you weren't a believer. Showing us how to fulfill his Great Commandment is what God is there for. That's what he's waiting for. Sometimes I think that's *mostly* what he's waiting for. On our own we can't properly love Normies — but with his help, we can't do anything but. And getting help from God is like getting help from anyone or anywhere else: It rarely if ever comes to us unless we ask for it.

Ouch

"I personally have extreme difficulty with the many Christians who seem almost obsessively compelled to bring Jesus into every conversation; it's really difficult to have a generalized, polite conversation with such people. I also know far, far too many Christians who are unabashedly vocal in their judgment of others, and who are incapable or unwilling to calmly and rationally discuss other religions or 'secular' points of view. I'm always impressed and happy to meet a Christian who not only knows anything about the history of their own religion, but who has also taken the time to learn about other religions. That almost never happens, though."

—M. K., LANCASTER, CA

"The one thing I would like to tell Christians about those of us who have chosen *not* to be Christian is that we aren't pagans in need of conversion. Some of us are rational adults, raised in fundamentalist, mainstream Protestant, or Catholic households, who have studied the Bible, attended Sunday school and church, and reached a point in our lives where we actively rejected one or more of the basic tenets of Christianity. 'Witnessing,' 'spreading the good news,' or otherwise telling me things I already know—and, in my case, have read in Latin, Greek, Hebrew, the original Aramaic, and in multiple English translations—won't make me change my mind about your belief system. It will simply drive a wedge between us. Jesus criticized the Pharisees for praying aloud in public and putting more emphasis on appearances than substance, and it seems to me that he'd similarly criticize many of the well-meaning Christians I run into who want to 'set me straight,' or help me find a 'personal relationship with Jesus.' I have a perfectly fine relationship with Jesus; I understand his teachings, and find much value in them. That I reject the religion that purports to promote his teachings doesn't make me a bad person; it just makes me a non-Christian. Nowhere in the Bible does it say that it's anyone's business to judge anyone else. Though I live in Dallas, I spend as much time as possible as far away from the Bible belt as I can get, in large part because of the rudeness of many of my neighbors regarding their religious beliefs. I think it might do American Christians some good to know that in cultures that are often assumed very similar to ours—in

New Zealand, Australia, and Canada, for instance — it's socially taboo to bring up religion in any but the most general context. In those places, to approach anyone — even someone you know well — and say, 'Are you saved? I'd like to tell you the good news about Jesus,' would be considered the very height of rudeness. It should be considered that here, too." —D. H., DALLAS

"Once Christians know I'm gay, the conversion talk usually stops. Instead, I become this sympathetic character who apparently isn't worthy of the gift of Christ. From my childhood in a Baptist church, I recall the 'loathe the sin, love the sinner' talk, but as an adult I can't say I've often found Christians practicing that attitude. Deep down, I'm always relieved to avoid disturbing 'conversion' conversations with Christians; discussing one's most intimate thoughts and personal beliefs isn't something I enjoy doing with random strangers. But at the same time, I feel as though Christians make a value judgment about my soul on the spot, simply because I am gay. I don't pretend to know the worth of a soul, nor the coming gifts to those who convert the masses, but I would guess converting the sinful homosexuals would merit a few brownie points. But I get the feeling that most Christians don't think we're worth the hassle." —R. M., HOUSTON

"If Christians would drop the Old World lore and superstition and stick with the very basic Christian principles — follow the Ten Commandments to find peace in your own life, be a good person without expecting immediate reward, accept that you are here for a reason and that you are exactly where you need to be, try your best to follow in the path of Christ — they would find a vast audience of people who could not help but agree with them, and would thus not need much else to be converted. It is when the ideals of Christianity get mixed up with the whole 'God is on our side' / 'You are either with us or against us' mentality that many people start to reject Christianity, even if they are in alignment with basic things like the Ten Commandments and the teachings of Jesus."—S. W., BERKELEY, CA

"I've never had a real problem with Christians in general, but I've always been tremendously uncomfortable with how often conversations about faith with 'devout' Christians boil down to their assertion that my beliefs are inherently invalid. When such Christians pull passages out of the Bible to justify marginalizing my own beliefs, I can't help but remember that 'even the devil can quote scripture.' I've never understood how or why Christ would have wanted me to come to him through the denial of my own thoughts and logic."—J. K., RICHMOND, VA

Talk Amongst Yourselves

What do you think of the proposition that the intention of Jesus' first miracle was to show that he loved and accepted people, exactly as they are? Why do you think Jesus chose to change that water into wine?

Do you think free will is more of a blessing or a curse? Doesn't it seem like it's a blessing because . . . well, because it means we don't have to be soulless automatons, but that it's a curse because it's the tool we most often use to separate ourselves from God?

Do you think it's possible to truly love someone without also respecting them? Would you want the love of someone who didn't respect you?

9

Normie, Can You Hear Me?

OKAY. SO NOW THAT you've gotten a Normie or two to trust you, it's *(finally!)* time to begin the conversion process. The first thing, of course, is to buy a pocket watch; after you've learned to swing the watch evenly to and fro, practice incanting in a low and soothing voice such phrases as, "You are getting sinful. Very, very sinful," and "Your life is a miserable failure. Nobody likes you. Only Jesus can save you. Call on the name of the Lord." When you think you've got the hang of it, invite your *Normie du jour* over for a late lunch, dim the lights a little, and get ready to chalk up another soul for God!

Well, that's it. I'm going to hell.

And all my Normie friends will be down there, going, "Ha! It was the *pizza*, wasn't it?"

And I'll say, "Oh, be quiet, fellow losers. It wasn't the pizza—though I doubt that helped. My Big Downfall was that I made this stupid joke about hypnotizing people into believing in God. *Moses* would be down here if he tried that joke. I was writing; I was hungry; this guy outside was screaming at his car . . . I just wasn't thinking. So what's there to do down here, anyway? Is it really OWWWWWW!!"

Luckily, here on earth we're free to Converse Away with our Normie friends uninterrupted, and sooner or later it's only natural that with those friends we'll get into at least a general conversation about our faith. And when a dialogue with any of our Normie buds dips that deep, we would do well to bear in mind how many non-believers have had the experience of getting fairly intimate with a Christian, only to have that Christian become disarmingly strident the moment the topic of religion or God comes up.

Or worse: The Christian, once he or she finds out that their Normie acquaintance has evolved opinions of their own about God and all the usual Spiritual Concerns, basically loses interest in the Normie, and is happy to let their relationship dissolve.

Back in my pre-Christian days, that happened to me all the time. I'd *think* I had a Christian friend—only, alas, to ultimately learn that what I really had was a fake friendship with a patient evangelist who, upon discovering that I had my *own* thoughts and ideas about God, determined in distressingly short order that I wasn't worth investing any more of their time in.

Man, that used to hurt.

So let's not do that! Let's be a *different* sort of Christian! Let's be the kind of Christian who goes into relationships with Normies assuming that those Normies already *have* fully developed thoughts, ideas, and convictions about God, religion, faith, and All Things Divine.

And let's go further than that! Let's be the sort of Christian who actually *respects* the spiritual views and opinions of others! Who actually listens to what non-Christians have to say about the very stuff that we feel so passionately *right* about!

Let's be the kind of Christian who actually *does* have non-Christian friends!

Ahhh.

Wouldn't that be nice?

No? The idea of respecting the religious views of non-Christians makes you clench your teeth a bit? Well, me too. Of course it does!

We're Christians! *We love our Lord and Savior, Jesus Christ! We sincerely want everyone in the world—and* especially *people we care about—to become Christian!*

Go, God!

Yet, the Fully Counterbalancing fact to our ever-present Everyone Convert imperative remains: We cannot be friends with a person—we can't really *love* a person—if we can't talk to them about God and religion without everything between them and us getting all tense and teeth-clenchy. And we better believe that if our Normie friend knows we're Christian, then in the course of a conversation with us about God they're going to be Particularly Alert to our becoming a tad more, shall we say, *zealous* than they might be altogether comfortable with.

It's a tricky conversation, basically.

Tricky, yet inevitable.

Like . . . falling in love. Or getting a cavity. Or losing one's . . .

You know what I think? I think that what *you're* thinking is that what we really need right here are . . . oh, I don't know . . . five Helpful Hints for successfully navigating through the tricky waters of our first real and deep conversation about God with a relatively new Normie friend of ours.

Well, say no more!

Five Helpful Hints for Successfully Navigating Through the Tricky Waters of Our First Real and Deep Conversation About God with a Relatively New Normie Friend of Ours

Hint #1: *Say No More*

Pretty much all any of us needs to bear in mind whilst talking to a non-Christian about Religious Stuff is the same thing *any* person does well to bear in mind whenever they're talking to any-one about anything, ever: *Listen.*

Listen, listen, listen, listen, listen.

Stop.

Talking.

Do you know that the older I get, the more I think that *the* single best thing you can say about someone is that they're a truly great listener? And I always wonder why being even a decent lis-tener is such a bizarrely rare personality trait. Maybe nowadays we all just spend so much time watching TV that when we're in a Real Time conversation, we just *can't* listen anymore — we're all listened out. Or maybe it's not a modern dysfunction; maybe people have *always* had trouble listening to others. Maybe cave-people were forever grunting and growling right over each other's not-quite-words. Maybe there's just something in our nature that makes it so that we can't stand it when, even for a moment, some-one else is in the spotlight that we can't help but feel *should* be shining upon us.

I know that's the one I'm always guilty of. Whenever someone else is talking, I always find myself thinking, "But you're taking up valuable time that could be filled with *me* talking. Be *quiet* already, won't you? So that I can say *my* fascinating thing?"

But in my heart of hearts, I know what we all know — that really *listening* to what another person has to say is the one sure way to show that person that you genuinely respect and care for them. (And listening to someone, of course, doesn't mean going mannequin on them: It means asking them questions about and encouraging them to elaborate upon whatever it is they've just said. Don't you *love* it when someone does that to you?)

When a Normie is sharing their ideas with us about God, they need to be heard. They need to know that we're open to what they're saying: that we're not judging it, or evaluating it, or (God forbid) pitying them for it.

And they *definitely* need to know that we're not just waiting for them to *finish* whatever they're saying, so that we can talk again.

Listening to one another is the *only* way relationships ever really grow stronger and move forward. We all know this. When we're talking to a Normie about God is sure not the time to forget it.

Hint #2: *Keep It Personal*

So if in our conversation with our Normie friend about God we've done our job, then sooner or later it will, in fact, be time for us to *(finally!)* talk. And the thing to bear in mind about that time is that we've got to make sure to keep in *personal* terms whatever we say about God, Christ, and the joys of our religion. It's a good and helpful thing for us to honestly relate how knowing Christ so benefits our lives; it's pretty Guaranteed Obnoxious for us to relate to another person how knowing Christ would benefit *their* lives.

"I just feel better about myself if I take the time to hear what God within me—the Holy Spirit—has to say about what I'm doing and how I'm acting," is one thing. "You'd just feel better about yourself if you'd take the time to hear what God within you—the Holy Spirit—has to say about what you're doing and how you're acting," is soooooo . . . something else.

The former indicates that the speaker is honest, real, and willing to be vulnerable; the latter indicates that the speaker is willing to use chloroform should they deem it necessary.

Talk about what knowing Christ has done in *your* life—how it affects *your* outlook, how it impacts *your* feelings about things. That's it. That's the pasture you're free to wander around in—but don't from there hop the fence, and start tromping around in fields you don't belong in. When it comes to talking about God with a nonbeliever, sticking with the strictly personal is the only way to make sure that the conversational door between the two of you continues to swing both ways.

Hint #3: *They've Seen the Light*

It's easy for Christians to slip into the belief that Normies have no experience or knowledge whatsoever of the divine. But that's like believing some kinds of fish just aren't as *good* in water as others—when, in fact, all fish are *great* in water, since that's their Native Medium. Well, it's the same with people: The fact that we all live in God's world means that every human on this planet is forever, in one way or another, listening and responding to God—whether or not they think in terms of "God" at all.

This is God's classroom; *everyone* gets called to the board. No one escapes The Big Questions: *Everyone* wonders who they are, where they came from, what happens to them after they die, how it can possibly be that so often water now costs more than soda, etc. Everyone wonders about God, and everyone has thoughts and convictions about God. Even atheists and agnostics have taken pains to position themselves relative to the whole concept and question of God.

We need to respect whatever it is that our Normie associates believe about God and the divine. Before I was a Christian, I had a lot of clear and firm ideas about who God was and how he worked, ideas born of a lifetime of feeling like The Big Divine had touched me, spoken to me, comforted me. One time, as a teenager in a strange home I was then having to call my own (I'd taken a job with these absurdly wealthy people as the live-in caretaker of their two toddlers), I went, lying in my little bed down in their basement, from being essentially paralyzed with grief and fear, to being deeply comforted by the settling over and in me of the reassuring presence of what I could only assume was God, come to rescue me. I didn't think of that warm presence as Christ—but it was surely no less comforting for that.

Another time, opening my eyes after meditating on a spot that overlooked the Pacific Ocean, I was again acutely aware of the presence of God within me. I didn't have to be a Christian to feel that—I just had to be a human being, paying attention. "The heavens declare the glory of God," says Psalm 19, "the skies proclaim the work of his hands. Day after day they pour forth speech; night after night they display knowledge. There is no speech or language where their voice is not heard."

There is no speech or language where the voice of God is not heard. Not a bad thing for we Christians to now and again recall.

God (or The Cosmic Mother, or The Great Nothing, or however they conceive of their version of the Almighty) is very real, and very seriously matters, to *all* people. We need to anticipate and respect the idea that any given Normie has views on a Supreme Intelligence, which they feel every bit as intensely about as we do our views on Jesus. Their conception of the divine reality may not be as defined as ours, but we *really* need to listen to them when they tell us about their relationship to whatever or however they think of God. And it *really* wouldn't kill us to at least be open to the idea that it's just ever so slightly possible that their conception and experience of God isn't as radically different from our own as we might at first be inclined to believe that it is.

Hint #4: *One Son, Many Stars*

Normies tend to think that all Christians are cut from the same (stiff, scratchy) cloth. I think it's a good thing for them to know that there are (almost) as many different kinds of Christians as there are kinds of people. There are over two hundred thriving Christian denominations in America today. Some are ultra-liberal; others are ultra-conservative; many are a mix of both. It's a big, varied world out there, and we're a big, varied faith. Some of us believe that homosexuality is a sin of behavior, the continued and unrepentant practice of which bars a person from heaven; others of us hold that God created homosexuals the same as he did heterosexuals, and that he doesn't care any more about a believer's sexual preference or orientation than he does the color of their hair.

Some Christians haven't a problem in the world with women clergy—they want *more* women clergy. Others hold that only men should head churches. Some believe that through Jesus is the only way to know God and get to heaven; others believe that the same uber-God introduces himself into different cultural streams at different times, in different places, and in different ways—but that it's the same God, and that every form of his expression and experience is perfectly divine.

While worshiping, some of us like to sing, dance, scream, and roll around on the floor; others of us you couldn't get to move with a cattle prod and a whip.

The bottom line is there are almost as many ways to be Christian as there are individual Christians. It's the single thing I wish more Normies knew about our faith. A lot of Normies stay away from Christianity because they *know* they're uncomfortable with one aspect or another of what they're so sure we all believe. What they very often don't know is that no matter who they are—no matter what their natural predilections, proclivities, or personality propensities—there's a style of Christianity that would fit them like a tailor-made suit. Very often people outside our faith just don't know that. I think it's awesome how many different ways there are to be Christian—and I think it's an aspect of who we are that's absolutely worth sharing.

Hint #5: *The Bible Didn't Tell* Them *So*

Wanna get a Normie to think you're insane and shut down on you like an abacus repair shop in Silicon Valley? Tell them that something is true because the Bible says that it is. We have *got* to remember that to a Normie the Bible *can't* be anything but a book written by people (and, Normies are usually pretty sure, people driven by a very clear agenda, at that). To them, *it's just a book.* We're free, of course, to talk with our Normie friends about what the Bible means to us in a personal or corporate sense—but at the same time, we have got to acknowledge that we fully understand how, to a non-Christian, there's barely any more reason to assume that the Bible is the genuine word of God than there is to assume the same thing about a phonebook, or the latest issue of *The New York Times.*

Finally—and this isn't a "hint" so much as a suggestion—consider the idea that sometimes love does, in fact, mean having to say you're sorry. If there's anyone in your life whom you at one time or another alienated by perhaps too fervently pressing your faith upon them, why not apologize to that person? Why not be honest with them, and tell them that by talking to them about Jesus, you really were just trying to share with them something that means so much to you, that the relationship you have with God brings you so much joy and peace that you're naturally motivated to share that with others—and that you were *especially* motivated to share it with them because of how much you like or respect them. Tell them that it's hurt you to think that what you said to them resulted in nothing more rewarding for either of you than a barrier going up between you, and how you'd very much like that barrier to come back down. Tell them that through thinking and praying about it, you've come to see that you basically blew it by being so enthusiastic about Christianity that you failed to properly hear or consider their own thoughts on such matters. Tell them that if they're willing, you'd at least like to be able to casually *chat* with them sometimes without there being all kinds of stress in the air between you — and that you promise to never, ever again try to convert them.

Tell them that in all honesty you'd be interested in sometime hearing some or more about what they think about God, or about what their experience has been with religion, or about what they do or don't believe in, Big Picture-wise.

Tell them you'd like to forget the past, and start again.

Man, I would have *died* if anyone who'd ever tried to convert me came back to me later and said anything like that. I'd have thought, "I don't care if this person *is* a Christian — they rock for saying that."

The thing is, you can be quite sure that your erstwhile would-be Christian will forgive you. People are just . . . good like that.

What God has joined together, let no man tear asunder, eh?

And unless I'm missing something, what God has joined together is every one of us with every single other person in our lives.

So it seems to me we'd do very well to apologize to anyone we've torn asunder from us — and *especially* if we did that in the name of the Lord, whom we love so much, and whom we so earnestly want to emulate.

Ouch

"When approached by a Christian who's trying to convert me, I find myself in an odd position. I hold a lot of the same values they do: that kindness is important, that to tend the sick and elderly is a human duty, that it is important to do good works. But we

differ greatly in regards to whether or not we think it's rude to try to push our beliefs on someone else. I view some 'hardcore' Christians with the same quizzical bemusement that I would someone claiming to direct their life by the prophecies of Nostradamus or Tarot cards—it seems alien and superstitious. And it definitely surprises me how often people overlook the teachings of Christ in order to focus on how to twist them into being exclusionary or hateful. If God created diversity, surely s/he would want her/his followers to accept it—let alone tolerate it. When Christianity is being used to create or reinforce ignorance, I find it truly frightening."
—C. R., REDMOND, WA

"I just don't understand how an organized movement to love one another became a crusade to tell the world, 'We're right, and you're wrong—and if you don't follow our way, then you're evil, and are going to hell.'"—Z. V., SAN FRANCISCO

"Most Christians are pretty good salesmen for Christianity; what they're not is good *examples* of Christianity. I had a good 'Christian' friend in college, for instance, who throughout the week used to have four different girls in and out of his dorm room—and who then sat in church every Sunday, declaring, 'Y'all need to get *right!*' It's as if Christians in general have a 'Do as I say, not as I do' mentality. What else can I think, when I see ministers living in multi-million dollar mansions and driving the most expensive cars—and yet preaching about how much Jesus loved the poor? I wish Christians would walk the good walk, instead of just talking the good talk."—C. B., ATLANTA

"I used to be a very hardcore Christian. (I eventually left the faith because I found that a God who would send people to hell was simply too cruel for me to believe in.) During the years after leaving the church, I came to realize what it's like to be on the non-Christian side of a conversion attempt. When you're on the Christian side of that exchange, you feel like you're helping the person avoid being thrown into fire. But when you're the non-Christian, it feels like the Christian is pouring gas all over you, mocking you with a match, and then, when you decide not to convert, tossing the match at your feet. It's no wonder communication between the two sides is nearly impossible."—S. W., PHILADELPHIA

"At least ten times when I was a child, my friends and I were approached by teens or men at a local mall, who would say to us something like, 'Hi, my name is John.' And I always dreaded the coming of what they *always* said next, which was: 'Did you know that Jesus loves you?' I am Jewish. I don't care if Jesus loves me—and if he does, I don't need to hear it from 'John' at the mall. I never push my Jewish values upon anyone, and would like it if people respected that, and didn't try to push theirs upon me. It is very abrasive; what religion I practice is none of anyone's business. And it's especially not the business of some stranger who comes up to me in a mall."—A. A., MIAMI

Talk Amongst Yourselves

Have you ever felt that the *primary* thing interfering with or constricting your relationship with a Normie was that they were not, or clearly did not want to be, Christian?

When Normies have what they would consider a "spiritual" or even religious experience—when they get that Indescribable, Inspiringly Peaceful feeling while, say, looking out at the beautiful view from atop the mountain they've climbed, or when holding their new baby for the first time — do you think that's Christ being with them? Even though they don't think of it that way?

How comfortable are you essentially recommending to others a strain of Christianity about which you personally have issues? In other words, if you're a conservative, or "traditional" Christian, and you're having a good, rich conversation about God with a nonbeliever whom you know is basically a leftist, "progressive" type, how comfortable would you be recommending to that person that they try attending a church that, say, every year enters a float in your city's annual Gay Pride parade? If, on the other hand, you're a hemp-wearing, dreadlock-sporting, gay-rights-advocating Christian, how comfortable would you be recommending to an Obvious Social Conservative a church that you know promotes an extremely conservative theology? In short, do you think it's better for someone to become *any* kind of Christian than remain no kind of Christian at all?

Do you think I'll go to You Know Where for making that opening joke about how Christians should *hypnotize* nonbelievers into believing? And if I do end up down there, don't you think the people I know there should at least *pretend* to be surprised when I show up?

10

Crazy? Who's Crazy?

IMAGINE THAT IT'S LATE one chilly winter's evening. You and your close Normie pals are sitting around a fire in the hearth: feet up, drinks in hand, dessert so perfectly satisfying you actually *don't* want any more. You're all feeling replete, content, and full of gentle goodwill. Life is good.

And then one of your companions says to you, "You know, [INSERT YOUR NAME HERE], you sure do an outstanding job of just loving us, and of never trying to convert us to Christianity. I know I speak for all the gang here when I say that if more people were like you, this world would be a much better place."

"Hear, hear!" says another friend, raising his glass to you.

"In fact," continues the first friend, "your unflagging personal kindness, consistent generosity of spirit, and dependable, proactive concern for the welfare of others have ultimately served to render me, for one, curious about your faith — about what exactly Christianity is, and what it means to you, and how it serves you. Would you mind, [INSERT YOUR NAME HERE], if I asked you some questions about your faith?" Looking around to the others, he then says, "And maybe some of you might also have a question or two about Christianity for [INSERT YOUR NAME HERE]?"

"Absolutely!" says a different friend. "You bet!" says another.

They all chime in: "Yes!" "Of course!" "Wonderful!" "I've got some real zingers in mind!" "I'll grill him like a steak!" "Oh, God! Finally! How I've yearned to learn about Jesus Christ! I'm so excited I think I'm about to have a nervous breakdown!!"

Now wouldn't that be a great moment? I mean, I hope everything works out for that last guy, but you know what I mean: If we really do become true and trusted friends with a nonbeliever, and they come to know and trust that we're not secretly counting the days before they join us in our faith, then it's likely that sooner or later they will ask us specific questions about what we believe, and why we believe it. And it would of course behoove us to have ready for such questions answers that at once truthfully represent what we believe, and that offer no support for the myriad misconceptions so many Normies often have about those beliefs.

We have a sane, rational religion. And that means that for any question we might get asked about it — and especially for those questions we're most typically asked about it — there's a solid, logical answer that would make clear, objective sense to anyone from an atheist shrink, to a Zen Buddhist, to Osama Been Hidin'.

By way of General Preparedness, then, please find following those questions or objections Normies most typically raise about our faith, along with what I personally think is (the gist of) a good, rational, non-alienating answer to each.

Your mission, should you decide to accept it, is to memorize each of the following questions, along with its answer. When in a conversation with you a Normie raises one of these questions, do not in your response fail to strictly adhere to the words of its corresponding answer. In the unlikely event that the given answers to two or more of the stipulated questions fails to instantly convert your Normie, do not panic. Request that your Normie remain where he or she is at, step beyond the range of their hearing, and call 1-800-NOGOGOD. That's 1-800 NO GO GOD. Trained evangelists will be standing by to advise you.

Oh, but hyuk.

No, but you understand: I'm not offering this Mini-Apologetic in the, "Okay, now that you've coaxed Hansel and/or Gretel into your candy cabin, *get 'em into the oven!*" kind of way. What I'm really saying is that the answers I'm offering to the following questions are the answers that I wish *I'd* gotten back when I used to ask Christians these very same questions—and they're definitely the answers I now give when I'm lucky enough to be asked such questions myself. See if you think you might find any of them useful in your own lives.

Q: I don't believe in God. Doing so just doesn't make sense to me.

A: Well, if there's one thing about this life we can say with absolute certainty, it's that God either does or doesn't exist. Either everything in the universe is created by some sort of over-arching, purposeful intelligence, or it's not. God or Mechanistic Coincidences: That's *it*, choice-wise. And determining that one of those two choices is more believable makes just as much "sense" as claiming the other is, since there's no way that any of us can empirically *know* which of the two is, in fact, the Right Choice.

Faith, whether in God or in no-God, really *is* a choice. And choosing either of the two makes perfectly good, perfectly sound sense. The fact is that we all better be comfortable with the truth that it's exactly as *reasonable* to assume that there is no God, as it is to assume that there is.

So why, then, choose that God exists? For Christians, that answer is simple: We believe in God because we *feel* the reality of him. For us, the God/No God scales *aren't* in balance; for us, they're fully tipped toward the side of there being a God. We don't believe in Christ because of something we read, or saw on TV, or even because that's what we were raised to believe; we believe because we don't know how *not* to, when our hearts and souls are forever telling us that God is real, and that he became a man called Jesus, and that Jesus died so that we could live free of the burden of our sins.

We choose God because we feel like God doesn't leave us any choice but to believe in him.

That said, though, what's also true is that, just on the face of it—and given the idea that anyone really *is* free to choose either way—it certainly seems more *fun* than not to believe that there is a God out there, watching over us, participating in our lives, trying to *tell* us rich, personal stuff all the time. It just seems a lot more . . . intriguing, to think that there's something Grand and Purposeful going on behind every last thing that happens in the world, rather than that there's not. If *nothing* else, believing in a God makes our whole system seem a lot more intrinsically or organically *human*, anyway; at the very least, choosing to believe in God seems, to we Christians, to be the difference between choosing a world that's in color and choosing one that's in black and white.

But getting to choose at all is, after all, why we have elections.

Q: Why doesn't God just *prove* he exists?

A: Well, to Christians (and, Christians would argue, to everyone) God *does* prove he exists, all the time. But what this question no doubt refers to is proof of the sure, objective, empirical kind that we usually associate with irrefutable factual knowledge. What someone posing this question is essentially asking is why God doesn't either appear to him or her personally, or, say, rent open the sky, and appear to everyone all at once.

What someone who asks for indisputable proof of God's existence is *really* asking is for their free will to be eradicated. They
don't want to *choose* to believe in God; they want to have no choice
whatsoever in the matter. The truth is, though, that no one who
doesn't already believe in God *really* wants new and conclusive
proof of God's existence. Because a person who suddenly has no
choice *but* to believe in God just got slammed into a very hard wall;
they just found out that for their whole lives they've been deeply
wrong about the most important thing in life. That's not a good
place to be. People should think twice before desiring to suddenly
find themselves there.

Q: If God's so good, then how come there's so much evil in
the world?

A: There's evil in the world because *people* do evil. What this
question always boils down to is, "Why doesn't God stop people
from doing evil?" The answer's simple: Because God loves us too
much to interfere with our free will to the degree that he'd have
to in order to remove from us the *choice* to do wrong. God gave
us our free will as *the* condition of our absolute independence: It's
what makes us human. (It's also how we *know* we're the Ultimate
Creation.) If God compromised our free will—if he stopped us
from doing *anything* we want to think or do—then we'd instantly
become something much less than human. We can't have it both
ways: We can't insist upon both our free will *and* upon a world
without evil. Evil is a *result* of free will: If we're going to make
choices, we're going to make bad choices, and bad things are going
to result. But as terrible as evil is, it's better than not having the
choice to do evil. It causes God unimaginable agony whenever we
do evil—but his love for us effectively binds him from controlling

or overtly interfering with our actions.

(Also, God couldn't stop acts of evil without stopping *thoughts* of evil. Because how would that work? How or when would our thoughts, feelings, or actions Officially Qualify as evil? Is it *evil* for you to think that your friend's new haircut makes her look like Bozo? If someone borrows money from you and doesn't repay it, do the thoughts that you then find yourself thinking about that person qualify as evil? If in a momentary fantasy you imagine stealing your money back from that person, is *that* a thought you'd like God to wipe out of your head before you even had it? You see the problem: You can't stop acts of evil without stopping thoughts of evil, and there's no applicable way to determine whether or not any given thought qualifies as "evil.")

Though it certainly seems contrary to reason and compassion, the fact that evil exists at all is actually definitive proof of God's supreme love for us.

Q: What about all the pain and suffering that's caused by "nature": diseases and hurricanes and so on? Why does God allow those things to happen?

A: Those things are bad, and do cause much suffering. But the truth is we won't ever know the extent to which we humans might be able to mitigate the damage caused by such occurrences, if we would only marshal our vast collective resources and focus them on addressing those concerns that *should* be common to us all, rather than waste so much of them fighting amongst ourselves. We've never, as one race, made our singular concern seeing what we might collectively be able to do to lessen the impact of all that trouble we call "natural." No fair looking to the sky for answers that might very well lie in our own hands, or hearts, or wallets. We've got to *really* cry in our hearts before we start crying to God.

Q: Christianity can't be any good, because look at all the corrupt, hypocritical Christians in the world—the crooked televangelists, the vile priests, the pastors who say one thing and do the opposite. And what about all the bad things Christians have done throughout history?

A: The reason there are so many Bad Christians is just because there are so *many* Christians, period. What group *doesn't* have its share of creepazoids and losers? What people outside the faith don't often understand is that all the good, sane, rational, kind, *normal* Christians are peacefully going about their lives; it's the crazy ones who get all the attention. But so what? Crazies always get attention. And yes, some bad Christians have always done some bad things—just as some people among any group of people always prove to be less than sterling characters. Just because someone does something in the name of Christ or Christianity doesn't make their actions Christian. The Bible teaches compassion, integrity, love, charity, and empathy; behavior contrary to these values isn't Christian behavior, no matter how many crosses the person doing them is wearing. If you judge that something you know a Christian to have done is abhorrent, then it probably is. But that doesn't mean Christianity is bad, any more than asserting that four plus four equals nine means math is irrational. Yes, within some historical contexts Christians have done some very bad things indeed; and it's undoubtedly the moral obligation of current-day Christians to rigorously (and humbly) denounce those things. But to be fair, let's also acknowledge that no other religion or group would even try to compete with the Christian record of building and running orphanages, schools, hospitals, food banks, charities, and countless social service agencies all over the world.

What's true about most Christians is the same thing that's true about most people: One way or another, they're all trying to improve. And that, right there, is the most any of us can dare to ask of any of the rest of us.

Q: All Christians ever seem to think about is sin. It's a sin to have premarital sex, to curse, to be gay, to watch certain movies . . . it's like they think it's a sin to be *human*. How can that be healthy?

A: Be gone, spawn of Satan! No . . . wait, wait: Scratch that response. The *correct* answer is: Yes, we Christians are indeed very concerned with sin—but not in the way that people usually think that we are. Perhaps we haven't been clear enough about making this distinction, but for Christians, sin isn't just the things people do—it's what people *are*. To us, being born human means that by our very natures we *must* sin; the tendency to be selfish, greedy, lazy, arrogant, nasty little sensation-grubbers—to, in other words, put our own needs before those of anyone else, including God's—comes absolutely hardwired into our DNA. (And, lest we forget, to a considerable degree it's also how we *survive*.) The kinds of behaviors that reflect so poorly upon us are caused by our being naturally programmed to behave in exactly those ways. That's what we mean when we say that people are born sinners: We really do mean *born*. Which means that all of us are also born destined to suffer the inevitable consequence of our "natural" sinning, which (among a lot of other awful consequences) is guilt. Guilt is natural to every human, because acting like a complete jerk is natural to every human. And for us, escaping from the interminable, cyclical nightmare of guilt and shame is where, thank God, Christ comes in.

Q: The god of the Old Testament is so vindictive and cruel. How can I believe in a god who behaves so terribly?

A: It's true enough that in the beginning our God was sometimes awfully firm with people. But to Christians, it's the same way parents sometimes must be firm with their young children. When kids are older, you can reason with them, and be subtler about your advice and guidance. But when they're toddlers, you sometimes have to simply insist that they pay attention, and that they behave in ways that you know are best for them. That's just life. And so at first God had to be as clear as necessary in order for everyone involved to (eventually) Get The Picture.

Additionally, it's not fair to select out for criticism only those episodes in which God seems to act harshly. A thorough reading of the Old Testament shows a God who is extraordinarily patient, wise, creative, and deeply loving. Moreover, the entire point of Jesus' coming was to eradicate the way things were done before that Mighty Fine Incarnation. That's why it's called the *New* Testament. Once Jesus arrives, it's a whole new ballgame.

Q: How is it that the Bible is supposed to be the infallible word of God? God didn't write the Bible—people did. Why should that book be any more the word of God than any *other* book people have ever written?

A: The idea of the Bible is that its entire production was guided by the Holy Spirit: its writings; its various translations; the thoughtful, rational, centuries-long process by which some books became part of its canon and others didn't—all of it. Christians believe that the actual, physical people who wrote the Bible did so while in the grip of the Holy Spirit. And it's important to remember that the Holy Spirit is *entirely* God: It's not a subset of God, or anything like that; it's the Whole Shebang. So Christians believe that the people writing the Bible were writing what God moved them to, that while working on it they were in effect minding God.

The Bible (comprising, for the record, sixty-six different books assembled from the writings of ancient Hebrews lost to time and early Christians we'll never forget), is a dense, heady mélange of historical narratives, stories about individuals, poetry, history, prophetic predictions, advice, prescriptions for observances, correspondences, direct declarations from God ... it's just *huge*, basically. Any book that old, large, and important is bound to engender infinite responses. Some Christians believe that every word in the Bible is the literal truth; others are content with the idea that some of its truths are expressed metaphorically. The one thing anyone who spends any time at all with the Bible is sure about is that there's a lot more going on with it than meets ... the I.

Q: If I can lead a moral life without Christianity, why do I need Christianity?

A: That Christians and non-Christians can't lead equally moral lives isn't the problem: They can. The problem is that what people very likely *cannot* do without Christ is to rid themselves of the guilt that results from all those times when they fail to live up to their moral standards—that is, from the self-imposed shame of their own sins. A sure way to eradicate the onus of personal guilt is the singular, glorious genius of Christianity. More than anything else, shame is what cripples the human soul; by his sacrifice on the cross, Christ, and Christ alone, lifts that shame away from all who believe that that's what he *came* to do. A person can certainly live morally without reference to the Christian God—but why settle for *only* being moral, when you can have morality *and* the clean conscience that comes from being forgiven? Especially given that nothing but nothing helps people to continue *being* moral than having a clean conscience?

Ouch

"I suppose that one of the things I find most frustrating about Christians is that I just can't bring myself to be one. I wish I could. Then I'd belong; I'd be part of the majority. But no matter how I look at it, I just can't make the contradictions of Christianity work for my life. I can't say, "Thou shall not kill," and then support all sorts of wars and violence — even if it is to defend my own country, my own religion, and my own children. I can't worship the Jesus who lived like a pauper, when the major symbol of his life — the pope — crowns himself in gold and jewels and eats like a king, while the majority of his subjects live in abject poverty. I can't ignore everything I know intellectually (like, say, about evolution), and simply replace it with faith — and so on and so on. So instead, all I can do is let my daily work and actions define my morality, and continue in my belief that the here and now is what I work to make it, and that all children — mine and others, of all backgrounds, and of all religions — are equally precious."
—G. A., SAN DIEGO

"It seems to me that today's Christians have taken the loving philosophy of Christ's teachings, and turned it into a policy of hatred and intolerance. If Jesus does return to earth, I think that many so-called Christians will be in for a very rude awakening."
—J. A., PHILADELPHIA, PA

"I have found that with most Christian evangelizers you simply cannot have a conversation based on logic. I'm not saying such people are incapable of logic or lack intelligence; the problem lies with the fact that they believe the Bible has inherent authority, and so base all of their arguments for their faith upon that conviction. For someone like me, who believes the Bible is merely a collection of mythological and literary stories, the Christian side of the debate becomes an *ipse dixit* argument. The last time someone effectively used the 'Because I said so' argument with me was my mother, and I was seven years old at the time."—M. D., BOSTON

"As a nonbeliever educated in the Scripture, I would say I would have much more respect for most Christians if they lived and preached the beatitudes of Matthew, rather than emphasizing the moralistic social dogma of St. Paul and the non-Gospel books of the New Testament. I also find that most Christians who try to evangelize don't have the knowledge of the Scripture they should, which leaves them unprepared to answer the tough questions about their religion."—B. S., SAN FRANCISCO

"Understanding and acceptance of *all* people needs to exist in order for the world to live in peace. It's 'Love thy Neighbor,' not 'Love thy Neighbor Only If They Share Your Beliefs.'"
—N. D., KANSAS CITY, MO

Talk Amongst Yourselves

Do you believe in "natural morality"—that a person can lead a perfectly moral life without in any way acknowledging or referring to any God at all?

Without regard to all the ways by which you *do* know God is real, what if any effect do you think it has on the ongoing reality of your faith that you can't, in any kind of empirically objective way, *know*-know that God is real? Do you think the fact that you can't *really* know helps your walk with the Lord, hinders it, or has no impact on it either way? Why?

Do you think a person can lead an emotionally satisfying life without ever having believed in Christ? In other words, when it comes to God, *is* ignorance bliss?

Now that this book has ended, are you going to have trouble carrying on with your life, since you know it's impossible for any book you will ever read again to be anywhere near as great as this one? Do you think it would be wise of you to start a support group with others who have read this book and subsequently been devastated by NOBWECS (No Other Book Will Ever Compare Syndrome)? What do you think of the multiple studies showing that one of the most effective ways to cope with NOBWECS is to buy a copy of the book you so loved for just about everyone you know? Do you think that is something that might work for you? Do you agree that this routine, which wasn't all that marvelous to begin with, is definitely running out of gas, and that I should just put an end to it right now? Why?

More Heart, Really, Than Appendix

(WATCH OUT – *THERE'S A BOMB!* Man, bomb jokes sure aren't what they used to be, are they? Too bad, cuz an Exploding Appendix joke right now could have been pretty yukkalable. But never mind.)

So I know that traditionally we Christians consider a fair number of Bible passages, besides the Great Commission, inspirations to get out there and try to convert a Normie or ten. Following are some of those passages; each is followed by my bracketed mini-response to it.

About those responses generally, let me say/repeat two things. First, I'm not ever at all meaning to in any way argue that the Bible doesn't tell us to evangelize; clearly, it does. All I'm saying (and what just about all my responses amount to) is that of *course* it was critical at the dawn of Christianity — back when the Bible was *written* — for everyone to get out there and convert up a storm. My humble contention is that in the Bible Christ and Paul are motivating believers to spread the Good News to people *who hadn't already heard it.*

And yay for their doing that! Verily, am I an unfettered fan of Our Man Paul. (Um. Though, that said, I think one of the most salient facts about Paul is that he was, to his bones, Just A Guy. Which is *particularly* why I like him — but why I also think that sometimes, every so often, it wouldn't kill us to ... remember that. But a book for another day, perhaps.) Today, though, most everyone in America has already heard the Good News. To continue to act as though they haven't is just . . . well . . . completely not working, if nothing else. And our failure to convert our neighbors matters, since (to repeat a point) the biblical call to evangelize isn't like other absolute, personal moral imperatives, such as those we find in the Ten Commandments. Implied in the directive to evangelize is to *succeed* at evangelizing, to actually win people to the Lord. Christ and Paul weren't telling us to get out there and *fail* at evangelizing. But failing to convert people is exactly what we're doing; worse, we're actually losing people. (See the Barna stats on pages 39–40 of this here tome.)

Add to our failure to convert nonbelievers the idea that by so zealously seeking to fulfill the Great Commission we are, in fact, working against the Great Commandment, and I think we've got ourselves a solid case for at the very least reconsidering some of the ways in which we currently represent and present our faith to all those nonbelievers in our lives who, we can trust, have already heard about, and already rejected, the Good News.

Anyway, here are some Bible quotes that Christians generally hold as spurs to evangelize, along with my understanding of them:

Acts 1:8

"But you will receive power when the Holy Spirit comes on you; and you will be my witnesses in Jerusalem, and in all Judea and Samaria, and to the ends of the earth."

[If a person feels an inclination or calling to travel to the "ends of the earth" to witness to someone *there* who hasn't yet heard about Jesus, then by all means they should go — and take with them the deepest prayers of all Christians. But here in America, where from sea to shining sea pretty much everyone already knows about Jesus, our Commission has already been largely accomplished. Here, it's basically over. We're done. At this point, our Good News is old news.]

Romans 10:13-17

"For, 'Everyone who calls on the name of the Lord will be saved.' How, then, can they call on the one they have not believed in? And how can they believe in the one of whom they have not heard? And how can they hear without someone preaching to them? And how can they preach unless they are sent? As it is written, 'How beautiful are the feet of those who bring good news!' But not all the Israelites accepted the good news. For Isaiah says, 'Lord, who has believed our message?' Consequently, faith comes from hearing the message, and the message is heard through the word of Christ."

[I don't read this as Paul exhorting all Christians, through all the time, to constantly evangelize; "How beautiful are the feet of those ..." doesn't sound to me like a universal call to action. It seems clear enough that here Paul is doing nothing more (and nothing less!) than selecting out for special praise those who were, back then, diligently spreading the Word. Also, I don't think, "How can they hear without someone preaching to them?" is terribly relevant for us today in America, in that Paul was talking about people who had yet to hear their first word *ever* about Jesus. Today, about the surest way to get a nonbeliever to *stop* listening to you is to start preaching at them. And (as unthrilled as I am to be taking exception to anything said by our esteemed Paul), faith doesn't come from hearing the message; faith comes from *accepting* the message. Whole other ballgame.]

2 Corinthians 3:2-3

"You yourselves are our letter, written on our hearts, known and read by everybody. You show that you are a letter from Christ, the result of our ministry, written not with ink but with the Spirit of the living God, not on tablets of stone but on tablets of human hearts."

[To my mind, this extraordinarily rich and elegant passage says: "Live like a true Christian; be sure that your heart, mind, and actions are wholly defined by the Spirit, rather than by anything having to do with legalism or dogmatism." It exhorts each of us to become the best Christian we can. If doing so inspires others to believe, then that's a magnificent form of evangelism. But I would argue that Paul is not here referring to the kind of active, aggressive evangelism to which so many nonbelievers these days so reasonably take offense. Paul is here telling us to *be* Christians, not to make Christians.]

2 Corinthians 5:19-20

"And he has committed to us the message of reconciliation. We are therefore Christ's ambassadors, as though God were making his appeal through us."

[Same as the above: This is about the personal, glorious state of *being* a Christian, and nothing beyond that. And, to be sure, every Christian is indeed an ambassador of God's. The function of any good ambassador, though, is to walk that fine line between properly representing their own country, and making clear how deeply they respect other countries and those who hail from them. An ambassador doesn't, for instance, make a point of trying to persuade people from other countries that his or her country is the *only* good one to live in or come from. Successful ambassadors — true ambassadors — are known for their ability to communicate sincere affection and respect for others. So if we're going to be Christ's ambassadors, then that's exactly what we should be communicating, too.]

Matthew 9:37-38

"Then he said to his disciples, 'The harvest is plentiful but the workers are few. Ask the Lord of the harvest, therefore, to send out workers into his harvest field.'"

[Again: Back then the "harvest" was indeed plentiful, since so few had yet heard of Christ. But in America today just about every last person has heard the Word; at this point, we're struggling to harvest plants that don't *want* to be harvested. Our American field simply doesn't need any more workers — and we should take care that those workers who *are* out there tread carefully upon the earth — that they behave in a respectful, considered way that is in general conducive to growth, rather than to its opposite. Our main concern these days should be nothing more intense or taxing than simply making sure that we don't stomp all over whatever wheat might still be out there, growing and being nurtured by the Son.]

Mark 4:26-29

"He also said, 'This is what the kingdom of God is like. A man scatters seed on the ground. Night and day, whether he sleeps or gets up, the seed sprouts and grows, though he does not know how. All by itself the soil produces grain — first the stalk, then the head, then the full kernel in the head. As soon as the grain is ripe, he puts the sickle to it, because the harvest has come.'"

[I think the telling part of this passage are the words, "though he does not know how. All by itself the soil produces grain . . ."To me, this says that people do not make converts, that that's *exclusively* God's doing. (Also, given that it seems clear enough the "man" here is a metaphor for Jesus, I frankly never understood how this passage is supposed to be saying anything at all about people going out to evangelize. I see it saying that Jesus everywhere makes his presence known—that Jesus "scatters seed on the ground." But we're not Jesus; surely it's not *we* who "put the sickle to it, because the harvest has come." I'm thinking that if instead of "a man," Jesus had meant, "*You guys* go out and scatter seed on the ground . . .," then that's what he would have said.)]

Matthew 5:14-16

"You are the light of the world. A city on a hill cannot be hidden. Neither do people light a lamp and put it under a bowl. Instead they put it on its stand, and it gives light to everyone in the house. In the same way, let your light shine before men, that they may see your good deeds and praise your Father in heaven."

[Here's what I understand this passage to say: "Be filled with me, and you'll be a true inspiration to others—who will then be moved to discover for themselves how you came about your superb character." Or just: "Know me; live right; be a beaming, eminently attractive example of my power." As far as I can tell, it's saying that by the authority of our example Normies are supposed to be drawn to us—not that we're supposed to go out and in any purposeful way take hold of them.]

1 Peter 3:15

"But in your hearts set apart Christ as Lord. Always be prepared to give an answer to everyone who asks you to give the reason for the hope that you have. But do this with gentleness and respect."

[Yes. Absolutely. We should be prepared to give an answer about our faith to *everyone who asks*. No question about that. But, again, I don't see this as directing us to in any sort of intrusive way talk about our faith with folks who haven't first asked to hear about it—and especially since doing that puts us at risk of compromising the respectfulness that Peter here admonishes us to maintain.]

John 15:16

"You did not choose me, but I chose you and appointed you to go and bear fruit—fruit that will last. Then the Father will give you whatever you ask in my name."

[I think the first sentence in this passage very, very carefully directs us to focus on the word "fruit." And having done that, I personally don't understand "go and bear fruit" to mean simply "go and convert nonbelievers." As far as I can see/feel/think, the directive here to "bear fruit" can mean anything from "become a superb parent," to "learn exhaustless patience," to "grow apricots as big as peaches." I don't see it as in any explicit or exclusive way meaning, "Go and convert people."]

2 Timothy 4:2

"Preach the Word; be prepared in season and out of season; correct, rebuke and encourage—with great patience and careful instruction."

[Now *this* is a clear call to evangelize. It's all I can do right now not to run outside and start flagging down cars. And I *would* do that, too — except that I know this passage is from a personal letter Paul wrote to his very dear friend Timothy, at a time when Paul was imprisoned and Christians throughout Rome were everywhere being violently persecuted by that ultimate zero, Nero. The palpable sense of urgency that marks this letter is born of Paul's eagerness to ensure the continued inspiration of Timothy; he *really* wanted to make sure that Timothy continued to spread the Word. And two thousand years later, let us all praise Timothy and the other early believers! Without their evangelizing, we'd all be . . . well, I guess that I, for one, would at this moment be charging outside in my pajamas to flag down passing cars. But today, there's no call for me to do anything like that. Again and again and again: Today, "all" I have to do, with all of my heart, is to love every last one of my neighbors, the same way God loves me.]

Acknowledgments

FOR THEIR INVALUABLE HELP and encouragement I am deeply indebted to my friend and agent Greg Johnson, my sheer blessing of an editor, Traci Mullins, and to my friends Kim Cohn, the Very Reverend Scott Richardson, Kim and Michael Flachmann, Rick Hornor, Rachel Barach, the Reverend Rhonda McIntire, and Pastor Martin Zimmann.

About the Author

JOHN SHORE is the author of *Penguins, Pain and the Whole Shebang: Why I Do the Things I Do, by God (as told to John Shore)*, and coauthor of *Comma Sense*, each of which won a 2006 San Diego Book Award (for, respectively, Best Spirituality/Religion and Best How To/Reference). A resident of San Diego, John has worked as an editor and/or writer for *San Diego Magazine, The San Diego Union-Tribune, The San Diego Weekly Reader*, and San Diego's public broadcasting station, KPBS. He has also published fifteen short stories in little literary magazines all over the country. John is a featured writer/blogger on the popular website Christianity.com. To visit John on the web, go to www.johnshorebooks.com.

HELP OTHERS EXPERIENCE GOD'S LOVE.

STOP WITNESSING ... AND START LOVING

Paul Borthwick   1-57683-233-3

Paul Borthwick helps Christians see that once they renew their own passion for Christ, the desire to share that life-changing love with the lost will soon follow.

LOVE WALKED AMONG US

Paul Miller   1-57683-240-6

People around the world know the name of Jesus, but few know his personal side. Discover the person of Jesus through an examination of the character trait that characterizes his entire life: his love.

DOWN-TO-EARTH DISCIPLING

Scott Morton   1-57683-339-9

Here's a practical, friendly guide to everything you need to know about one-to-one discipling without terrifying you or those you want to reach. It divides the process into simple, manageable steps based firmly on biblical principles.

Visit your local Christian bookstore, call NavPress at 1-800-366-7788, or log on to www.navpress.com.
To locate a Christian bookstore near you, call 1-800-991-7747.